GLADLY LERNE, GLADLY TECHE

Hugo Brown: Headmaster 1936-1971
(by courtesy of H. Tempest Ltd.)

GLADLY LERNE, GLADLY TECHE

Memoirs of the First Thirty-Five Years of Croftinloan School

1936–71

by
HUGO BROWN

First published by Foxbury Press, 1 Step Terrace,
Winchester in 1990

© Hugo Brown 1990

ISBN 0 946053 02 2

Typeset by J&L Composition Ltd, Filey, North Yorkshire
Printed in Great Britain by Henry Ling Ltd.,
at the Dorset Press, Dorchester, Dorset

CONTENTS

LIST OF PLATES
(between pages 48 and 49)

FOREWORD

It is a privilege and pleasure to be asked to write a short foreword to *Gladly Lerne, Gladly Teche*.

I have been fortunate to know Hugo Brown for nearly 60 years. As a young schoolboy at Ardvreck I remember him as strict but patient and always fair. His wise guidance towards the Christian way of life has been a great benefit to many of his former pupils and his great interest in every schoolboy he taught is something both boys and parents will always remember. It is not surprising that at an early age he became Headmaster of Croftinloan. After a modest start, the school developed into one of the leading preparatory schools in Scotland. The solid foundation he has established will be a benefit to many generations to come. He will claim that much of the success of the school has been due to a team effort but he was the captain of the team.

Having had four sons at Croftinloan, I am one of many parents who are grateful to Hugo Brown for his outstanding guidance. His is a fascinating story and will be of great interest, not only to those who have had some connection with Croftinloan but to many others who enjoy an interesting story of enterprise and enthusiasm written by a talented schoolmaster. The challenges he encountered are numerous and the humorous incidents he relates add to the enjoyment of the book.

I would like to congratulate Hugo Brown on a job well done.

Sir Eric Yarrow, M.B.E., D.L.

INTRODUCTION

The decision to write this book was made some years ago but only now has it appeared in print. I am grateful to the persistence of many friends who pushed me along by frequently enquiring when it was likely to be published. I hope they will not be too disappointed at the result.

I am especially indebted to those Old Boys who responded so enthusiastically to my request for material for the book. With uninhibited frankness they have given differing accounts of their reaction to life at Croftinloan when they were there. Some of these contributors maintain that they were 'rebels' when at school. I have tried not to be too selective and hope that those who have placed themselves in that category will feel that they have been given fair representation.

I am most grateful to Sir Eric Yarrow for writing the Foreword. His long association with the school as a parent and governor has been an exceptionally happy one and his advice and encouragement to me, personally, have been enormously helpful.

Thanks are due to my wife for typing the manuscript – particularly when this involved a good deal of deciphering – and for gently but firmly suggesting alterations to the text; to Mr Robert Cross, the publisher, for his guidance and patience and to Mrs Ramsbotham, the editor, for her many useful suggestions. I would also like to thank the proprietors of the *Perthshire Advertiser* for permission to reprint several photographs.

In conclusion, I must refer to the school's state of health in 1990. Under the headmastership of Sir John Maclure and supported, so ably, by his wife, Croftinloan continues to prosper. A great many improvements have been carried out and new buildings have made it possible for more pupils to be accommodated. In spite of the increase in numbers, however, the importance of a family atmosphere is still considered to be of vital importance – one in which Christian standards can be sustained and fostered.

11th April 1990   Hugo Brown

CHAPTER 1

DAYS OF PREPARATION

My boarding-school education began at the age of twelve in a Scottish Preparatory School. After I had made the lives of several governesses pretty miserable, my parents decided, probably rightly, that I needed the discipline of a boarding-school. I do not think that they approved wholeheartedly of boarding-schools but their decision proved to be a good one. At the time, I did not see it that way; in retrospect, I only wish they had made it earlier.

I crept very unwillingly to school. I was certainly the oldest New Boy and suffered for it. The experience has made me very sympathetic towards those who leave home for the first time in their teens. Once I settled down, however, I looked upon my prep school as less and less of a Squeers establishment and thoroughly enjoyed my last few terms.

My parents then decided to send me to an English Public School in Somerset – one which they knew well by repute and in which there was quite a number of Scottish boys. I had, of course, to sit an Entrance Exam and, to my surprise, was placed in a fairly high form. Though French and English were my strong subjects, I was not really, at that time, academically inclined, being more interested in the playing-field than the classroom. However, my Headmaster thought I was of University material so, after my Maths master had performed a miracle on me, I succeeded in entering Cambridge University to read Modern Languages at Christ's College.

It was not until my third year at University that I thought I would like to teach in a boys' preparatory school – preferably in Scotland. So, after graduating, I remained at Cambridge for a fourth year (or, as it turned out, for part of a fourth year) in order to go to a Teachers' Training College run by a gentleman of the name of Fox (we were, rather unfairly, dubbed 'Fox's Martyrs'!). Most of my practical work was carried out at the local Perse School, which was very much ahead of the times in its teaching methods. I was more than fortunate to have MM Chouville and de Glehn as my instructors. Sometimes they were almost brutally frank in their criticism but this was good for me and I respected them for their outspokenness. It was a little daunting to see them sitting at the back of the class as I did my inadequate best to reach the standard they expected of me. They were both most helpful and I owe a great deal to them for their patience and encouragement.

I had fully intended to complete the course, although I was more than a little apprehensive about my ability to satisfy the examiners on the history and theory of education. I was much more interested in the practical aspect of teaching. However, I need not have worried.

I had a cousin who was friendly with the Headmaster of a Scottish prep school and, knowing that I would shortly be looking for a teaching post, asked him whether he had any vacancies on his staff. He replied that there would be an opening for a teacher of French. 'Well', replied my sponsor, 'I know a young man who is looking for such a post, but I do not think he will be available until after he has finished the course he is taking'. I was approached and, ultimately, interviewed and accepted. I had a difficult decision to make but, feeling that the examiners might not be too happy about my lack of knowledge of the history and theory of education, I wavered. When, however, I was invited to coach the Rugby team, I felt it much easier to make up my mind! In telling the boys that I was a University Blue, however, the Headmaster was misinformed: though I had represented my College for four years, was a member of the 'Sixty Club' and had played for leading clubs in Scotland and England, I had no qualifications, apart from enthusiasm, for coaching Rugby.

I began work at Ardvreck, Crieff, in the summer of 1931, hoping that the short time I had spent at the Training College would at least prevent me from disgracing myself when faced with critical schoolboys, eagerly looking for chinks in the new master's armour. At the end of a day's teaching I felt completely drained, but I suppose that is the experience of most beginners. I must say that I sometimes found it difficult to agree with the Oxford Cleric in *The Canterbury Tales* of whom it was said 'Gladly would he lerne and gladly teche', but I was glad that he stated his aims in that order. I was certainly learning but was I teaching? One of my pupils did very badly in the Common Entrance Examination for Glenalmond at the end of my first term and the boy's last. The Headmaster was generous enough to say: 'Well, Brown, you've not been here long enough to ruin the French. I have arranged for you to take the boy to Glenalmond for an interview'. I felt I, too, was going to be interviewed. Fortunately, for both pupil and master, the boy was accepted – I thanked God and took courage!

After four and a half years at Ardvreck I felt, with the arrogance of youth, that I was no longer a novice and that I was now equipped to climb further up the ladder. My ambition was to 'found' a new preparatory school in Scotland. I never thought this would be easy but I did not expect it to be the uphill struggle that it turned out to be. Our school motto, *J'ai bonne espérance*, had been well chosen.

CHAPTER 2

SEARCHING AND FINDING

Very fortunately for me, I had some influential sponsors who seemed to be as keen as I was on the idea of setting up a new school. These included Professor Albert Carless; Mr R. C. Greig; the late Lord Maclay; Mr George W. Service; Mr W. H. P. Sloan; Sir John Roxburgh; and my own preparatory school Headmaster – Mr F. W. Gardiner. It was, however, my father who initiated the whole venture and gave me so much support and encouragement. Being a Chartered Accountant he dealt with all matters relating to finance. His death just three weeks before the school opened on 7th May 1936 was a very great blow to my sister and to myself, but we were fortunate in having Mr Sloan (who became the first Chairman of the Governing Board), Mr G. W. Service, and the other Governors to turn to for advice.

Starting a new school is a rather tiring and protracted exercise but the moral and practical support given by those already mentioned, and by a host of others, was of immense help to me as, together, we searched for suitable premises. Many properties were looked at but, for a number of reasons, turned down. One on Loch Lomondside appeared initially to be ideal, and I really thought that we had come to the end of our searching. However, my father quietly remarked that if we selected premises so close to a loch, the new school might well gain undesirable notoriety! The warning was heeded and the search continued.

The trail eventually led to the Pitlochry area. The estate in which we were particularly interested was situated two miles south of Pitlochry and had been on the market for a number of years. It was described as having originally been owned by a member of the Atholl Fergusson family, and subsequently the property of Admiral Jack Murray. The present owner, Mr Paterson-Brown of Edinburgh, had acquired the estate of 130 acres in 1927 from Mrs Gwyer, who lived at Croftinloan for around fifty years.

When my father, Mr Sloan and I arrived to see over the building and the estate, the three gardeners, John Watt, his son Willie and Alistair Carter, were standing at the front door, seemingly at attention. We were an hour late and admired their patience and endurance. (Perhaps these qualities were accounted for by the fact that John Watt was a veteran of

the Boer War and later a Sergeant-Major with the Scottish Horse.) We
heard afterwards that John's daughter was to be married that afternoon,
though he succeeded in hiding the anxiety he must have felt as we slowly
went round the mansion, asking what we considered relevant but, from
his point of view, rather time-consuming questions. He gave us a
foretaste of his pawky humour that day. Whenever he came to a
bathroom he would open the door and announce: 'Another house of
refuge!'

It did not take us long to come to the conclusion that the search was
over. However, Mr Sloan, looking up at the big 'pile', remarked that
possibly a smaller building would have suited our purposes better. A few
years later we wished it had been larger. The house and grounds had
many points in their favour. Unlike most of the other properties we had
seen, there was sufficient flat ground near the house which could be
utilised for games; the interior could be readily adapted for school
purposes; the estate was within easy reach of Pitlochry, which was itself
in the very centre of Scotland. Lastly, and most importantly, it was
superbly situated with a beautiful view of the Tummel valley. As a
bonus, there was a tenanted farm, and we had hopes that the boys –
particularly those from urban areas – might profit by helping there.

The scene now moves to a classroom at Ardvreck where one hot day in
June 1935 some small boys were being taught the elements of French. A
knock at the door was a welcome distraction. The Headmaster's butler
entered and handed me a telegram which I quickly opened, my hands
shaking a little. Mr Wooff waited to see if I had any reply to make after
reading the contents, but as none was forthcoming he left the room. The
boys were naturally curious – particularly as they noticed I was smiling.
'Good news, sir?' one of the bolder ones asked. 'Yes', I replied, 'Very
good news! A rich uncle of mine who lived in Australia has just died and
left me his entire fortune.' The telegram from my father was brief and
very much to the point. It read: 'Offer for Croftinloan accepted'.

Later, I felt rather ashamed of this massive piece of deception but
comforted myself with the thought that probably very few, if any,
believed me! However, if Eric Yarrow, Andrew Pettigrew, David Greig or
Jock Young were in that class on that day and heard me lie so blatantly, I
hope they have forgiven me. The gullible no doubt broadcast the good
news that I would probably be leaving at the end of the term as I no
longer had to earn my living as an impecunious schoolmaster.

CHAPTER 3

A RACE AGAINST TIME

The first part of our dream had been realised but a great deal of hard work lay ahead. As far as I am aware, Mr Paterson-Brown and his wife lived in Edinburgh during the winter months and only occupied Croftinloan for a few months of the year. Consequently, there was no central heating in the building. Our first task was to have this installed on a limited scale, intending to extend it when funds became available. The young are not supposed to feel the cold but in large dormitories, with high ceilings and badly-fitting windows, the boys certainly would. We were not yet on the National Grid and a small Petter engine was called upon to supply all our heat and light. With a voltage of only 110 we were very much restricted in our use of electrical appliances.

When the alterations began, in September 1935, it seemed that May 1936 was a very long way off, but we needed every minute of the time available. In the belief that when workmen are in a house the owner should be very close at hand, I lived in the building during the nine months of renovation. I cannot say that I enjoyed the experience, as the noise and dust reduced my spirits to a very low ebb at times. On top of this were the daily frustrations. Though the men on the job worked extremely well they were often held up by the suppliers. During those never-to-be-forgotten months, my housekeeper, Mrs Edward, looked after me well, cheering me up when I was down, though I expect she was often rather dispirited herself. Living in a large, draughty mansion for that length of time can be no one's idea of paradise.

One of the biggest tasks was the preparation of what was to become the playing-field. It extended to around three acres and had not been cultivated in any way since the First World War, when I understand it was under potatoes. I should have hired mechanical cutters but John and Willie Watt insisted that, though it would take time, they could easily scythe the extensive area by hand. This was but an early indication of the character of these two stalwarts – nothing was ever too much trouble for them. When Willie was called up at the beginning of the War we soon realised how indispensable he had been. As we grew a lot of vegetables we tried to get him into the 'reserved' occupation group, but our attempt failed: the walled garden, in the opinion of the authorities, was not quite large enough to permit us to retain his services. John Watt carried on for a time unaided, but later we were able to get a local Land Girl to help him.

No levelling had to be carried out on the field except in the area which was to become the cricket square. The work was supervised by Mr Joe Anderson who owned a sports shop in Perth. He had the distinction of scoring a century when playing for Scotland against the Australians, and was also a fine bowler. We were indeed fortunate in being able to engage 'Joe' as our first cricket coach.

It was a great day when my sister Helen arrived from Craigflower Preparatory School, near Rosyth, where she had been Matron under Mr and Mrs Frank Wailes. By the time she arrived on the scene, most of the workmen had packed up and gone but they had, unavoidably, left behind them a great deal of dust and rubble. When my sister saw the mess her heart must have sunk. However, she immediately started the mammoth task of making the building habitable, receiving most valuable assistance from Jeannie Macfarlane, daughter of the tenant farmer, who later married Alistair Carter. By their energy and efficiency they transformed the building. A notice was put up at the Lodge gates: we were now open for business! My sister threw away her duster and assumed a number of offices – Hostess, Housekeeper, Matron, to mention but three. Over the years she was to develop a wonderful rapport with the boys and their parents and played a major part in the growth and success of the school.

CHAPTER 4

THE GREAT DAY

I do not know whether 7th May 1936 is engraved on my heart but it is certainly inscribed on my memory. On that day, three small, apprehensive boys arrived at Croftinloan to begin a new life and to make history. I am not sure whether the first boy to be entered for Croftinloan actually arrived first but he was probably less fearful than the other two, as his home was in Pitlochry and playing truant would have presented no problems. Probably Blair Macnaughton was not consulted in the matter but I did admire the courage of his parents in deciding to take such a leap in the dark by entering him for a school which was about to begin its very first term. Little did we know then that Blair was to play such an important part in the development of this new venture. Eventually he had two sons and a step-grandson at Croftinloan and became a governor and later vice-chairman of the school Board. His practical interest, through fair and foul weather, will never be forgotten.

Number two was a grandson of Mr George Service, one of the early governors who, like Mr W. H. P. Sloan, was a Glasgow shipowner. I cannot remember Anthony Service having been officially entered. Perhaps, in view of his grandfather's position, he just turned up on the 7th! He brought a good deal of colour into the life of the school and we were not surprised that he, later, entered the theatrical world. It could justifiably be said that he had a foot in it when still at Croftinloan. He showed early signs of promise by borrowing my cap and gown and walking majestically into the library, carrying a large Bible. He then proceeded to conduct a service with great aplomb and reverence. Unfortunately, like many of us, he did not always practise what he preached. He established quite a reputation for himself as an After-Lights speaker and, once he got going, it was almost impossible to silence him!

Robert Buchanan completed the trio. He was the son of a doctor in the West of Scotland and his rather broad accent left one in no doubt as to his 'provenance'. He was a cheerful, helpful boy and the fact that he was one of three did not, as far as I can remember, result in any serious internecine warfare as is sometimes the case with trios.

And so our little family of three, founder-members of Croftinloan, took over a very large house which it was to occupy for the next three or four years. It must have been an extraordinary experience for them to wake up on the morning of 8th May 1936 in such strange surroundings and to realise that, apart from the members of staff, Tom Kirkwood (of whom more later) and myself, they were the only occupants of the large building. Only one to my knowledge shed any tears. I remember that Anthony was quite upset as Blair had declared that he intended to marry Valerie – Anthony's sister – when the time was ripe! Whether this was a threat or love at first sight (she may have accompanied her brother to school on the 7th) I am unable to say, but the possibility did cause Anthony some anxiety. He must have considered Blair as a most unsuitable brother-in-law.

The question uppermost in our minds was: 'Will we ever be able to persuade a sufficient number of parents to believe that Croftinloan is going to be one of the best prep schools in Scotland?' If we could have persuaded, say a round dozen, to enter their boys, momentum would have been created and expansion would have resulted. So many said, very understandably, that they liked what they saw of the school but, frankly, wanted to send their boys to a larger establishment where they would be able to participate in organised games and communal activities. I have known schools being started with a small nucleus of boys but we did not have that advantage and, indeed, one boy was removed because of the slow growth of the school. This was a bitter blow at the time but, later, we were to realise that there was some advertisement value in the decision made by the boy's parents because they sent him back to Croftinloan when the numbers had increased!

Our local minister, the Rev. Charles Hepburn, who, along with his wife, was so interested in our venture, suggested that he might write an illustrated article. He took a great deal of trouble over this and submitted the article to the *Scottish Field*. The editor returned it with one of his very polite letters and we were not altogether surprised. We would have to think again.

We remembered the school motto, and the crest depicting a knight in armour, moving into battle with a broken lance. Was he another Don Quixote, tilting at windmills, or was he on a crusade? We thought the latter and we shared his crusading spirit. We knew we had a battle on our hands and we badly needed some reinforcements.

CHAPTER 5

TEETHING PROBLEMS

Obviously, we had to produce a prospectus but, initially, whilst the school was still in embryo, we decided to get a pamphlet printed, giving the barest details. Possibly this was a mistake but, if it was, we soon put it right by bringing out what we thought was a very attractive prospectus, profusely illustrated. I treasure the one copy in my possession. By the standards of these days the format was good but some of the reading matter makes one smile some fifty years later: 'The school is lighted by electricity'; 'Every boy has a warm bath three times a week and a cold bath every morning unless forbidden by the doctor or by his parents'; 'During the rest period, all boys lie flat on their backs and a master reads to them'; 'The masters take an interest in everything which interests a boy and, whenever possible, join in all the games'; 'Each boy when he returns to school deposits his money in the school bank. Five shillings a term is a good average allowance'; 'No boy may return after the holidays without a Health Certificate'. An Old Boy, who is now Headmaster of an English preparatory school, says that he was quite amazed at the extraordinary precautions taken to prevent an infectious disease from spreading. Probably he did not realise that we were, in fact, following the recommendations of our 'Trade Union' (the I.A.P.S.). In those days schools, by and large, followed the directives of the Council, though today it is not unusual for a school to 'do what is right in its own eyes'! Nevertheless, it must have seemed a little unnecessary to isolate the school from the larger community. Though this anonymous O.C. (Old Croftinloan) says that he did not notice disinfected straw at the school gates, he adds that he would not have been surprised if the letters the boys sent home had been fumigated. The school was in quarantine for weeks, he records, as the current 'pox' picked off the inmates one by one. His father came to take him out at the weekend during a period of enforced seclusion and was told that sledging was only permitted beyond Ballyoukan Lodge (a school boarding-house, a quarter of a mile away) where no living soul would conceivably be loitering. Although I must not doubt the veracity of an I.A.P.S. Headmaster it seems to me that hyperbole has to a certain extent triumphed over accuracy...

We had not been at Croftinloan for very long before another problem presented itself and, over fifty years later, it has not yet been completely solved. I refer to the private water supply which was collected mostly from the 'Birch Park' – a 50-acre wood above the school. The static water, amounting to some 6,000 gallons in 1936, was barely adequate for a household of ten and, as the school grew, it would become totally inadequate. It was fortunate that I got to know the keeper on the neighbouring estate (Mr Foot) who knew every inch of the moor above the Birch Park – outside our territory. One day we set out on a search for water and, leaving the Birch Park behind us, Mr Foot introduced me to an area of moor about 100 yards from the Croftinloan/Donavourd boundary wall. He pointed out to me some springs – three in all, I think – which he said had never gone dry in his lifetime, adding that he was sure that the Maxwells, who owned the estate and were good friends of ours, would allow us to tap that source. There was no difficulty; we paid our 5s per annum to the Donavourd Estate and ran a pipe from the moor to the collecting tank in the Birch Park. This certainly improved matters, but in very dry spells (a rare occurrence in Scotland!) the boys had to be economical. At Ballyoukan Lodge, where Edward and Jean James were in charge, the boys were told not to leave any taps running. Edward then added: 'If you do, you may have to be sent home'. From the comparative safety of South Africa, John Rollason writes to tell me that this possibility cheered him up tremendously and that he and his collaborators left the taps running deliberately. To their chagrin they never succeeded in making their Housemaster implement his threat! I look upon this 'bolshie' behaviour as but a temporary lapse on the part of John, who later became a prefect and an excellent Head Boy.

We were rather anxious about what would happen should a disgruntled pupil set the school on fire, as 6,000 gallons would not go very far. We did, in fact, have a small fire in the early days. Asleep in the dormitory, James Hamilton was awakened by the smell of burning. He leapt out of bed and woke up the most senior boy, but was told to shut up and go back to bed. To James's credit, he refused to obey his 'superior' and made his way, speedily, to my sister's room to raise the alarm. On investigation, it was found that a fire had started beneath the grate of our sitting-room fireplace – just above Jim's dormitory. I was called. The Fire Brigade was called. The boys did not need to be called – they did not want to miss any of the drama, for here was something worth recording in their Sunday letters. It was also something for the local Press to exaggerate and they made the most of it. I am not sure whether Jim Hamilton was looked upon as a hero or as a 'scab'!

When the Swimming Pool was built in 1954 the 40,000 gallons which it was said to contain would have been able to extinguish larger fires than the one described. For quite a while, until we could get the dormitory ceiling re-decorated, the small blackened mark caused by the fire was evidence of a boy's quick thinking and perhaps of our lethargy in removing that mark. Prospective parents seeing over the school would often look ceilingwards with a quizzical glance – to be told that the mark was caused by a small fire did not always seem to re-assure them! We hastened to inform them that, in consultation with the Fire Brigade, we had regular fire-practices. (I must admit, however, that the ladders and other forms of escape were rather primitive compared with what is now required by the authorities.) Most boys enjoyed these practices, but a few were scared stiff by them and had to be introduced very gently to the 'drill'. However, even the least enthusiastic admitted, once the practice was over, that an hour spent in this way was preferable to an hour spent in the classroom. When, on rare occasions, the practices took place after Lights Out, we found that the very loud alarm bells failed to waken the heavy sleepers such as Alisdair Cockburn, whom an earthquake would not have disturbed.

CHAPTER 6

A TURNING POINT

We were very grateful to the friends we made locally. They encouraged us in every possible way but there was a limit to what they could do. It was clear that we must widen our circle, particularly in the educational field where influence lay. Before we had time to follow up this idea someone, who was to become a very good friend of Croftinloan, made the first move and this is how it happened.

When Croftinloan opened, Canon Mathewson was Warden of Trinity College, Glenalmond. I had met him when I was an assistant master at Ardvreck and as a large number of boys from that school moved on to Glenalmond, I attended several functions there. However, it was not until I became Headmaster of Croftinloan that I got to know the Warden well and over the years a strong link with the College was formed. For many years, more Croftinloan boys went on to Glenalmond than to any other Public School.

A number of entrants from other schools had failed the Entrance Examination to Glenalmond, but the Warden was prepared to give them a second chance. Knowing that our numbers were small, he suggested to the parents of these boys that they should get in touch with us. Several did so and, after seeing over Croftinloan, entered their boys for a term or two. They were not dull boys but simply had not covered the syllabus required for the C.E.E. One boy, who was highly intelligent, got exceptionally high marks when he re-sat the examination, and all passed. Their parents were naturally delighted and broadcast their pleasure. This was a great encouragement to us – we seemed to have broken through at last.

This contact, once established, was followed up and strengthened. I made frequent visits to Glenalmond, although I felt a bit of a scrounger at times, and was always made most welcome, provided I did not interrupt the Warden at his hobby – that of making relief maps. I remember seeing a number of these on display in his study. Behind one of these, hanging on the wall, was a notice which read: 'Tobacco is a filthy weed but I love it'. Such a statement might, today, have been given less prominence!

Canon Mathewson did cause me some embarrassment at times. He often used to introduce me to parents as 'the man who gets boys through the Common Entrance Examination'. I suppose I accepted the compliment readily enough, but had he known the truth he would have realised that my second-in-command, Tom Kirkwood, was largely responsible for our examination successes. Tom was a contemporary of mine at Cambridge where, although not at the same college, we became firm friends through the Cambridge Inter-Collegiate Christian Union, of which we were both active members. After teaching at Croftinloan for a while from the outset, Tom took on greater responsibility and joined the staff at Millfield.

Grateful though we were to Canon Mathewson for his help when we were struggling, we were equally grateful to subsequent Wardens – particularly to Christopher Smith and Ralph Barlow, both of whom became close friends. The latter maintained a strong link with Croftinloan over many years and performed the opening ceremony of the Swimming Pool in 1954 and that of the Assembly Hall in 1961, the year of our Semi-Jubilee. I remember his asking me as he stood by the side of the Pool whether he was expected to dive in. I assured him that I had appointed a deputy in the person of Frank Gerstenberg, the Head Boy at that time and now Headmaster of George Watson's College, Edinburgh, to undertake this duty. Mr Barlow was greatly relieved. Frank carried out his duty with a dive worthy of the occasion. Many years later when the Pool had been covered in and heated, the occasion was marked by a similar but more dramatic dive when one of the parents took to the water, fully dressed. It looked very much to me as if he had been 'helped' on his way! The suit he was wearing was clearly an old one.

The residents of Pitlochry and of the neighbourhood looked on with interest as the struggle to increase numbers continued. Mr and Mrs Maxwell of Donavourd House – our immediate neighbours – continued to be most helpful and friendly. They were the first people to call upon us in 1935: I suppose a mixture of curiosity and a desire to be friendly brought them along so that they might meet the crazy schoolmaster who had embarked on such a venture at a time of national and international financial crisis. They showed very practical interest in what we were trying to do. Their help with our water problem has already been mentioned but they went even further – we swopped cars: the Maxwells bought my Wolseley and I bought their large Dodge estate car, which resembled a house on wheels. Little did we realise at the time that the running of such a large vehicle with its insatiable appetite was going to present us with another problem when war broke out and petrol was rationed but, sometimes, it is folly to be wise. The Dodge gave us enormous pleasure; could transport seven or eight people at a time and, generally, did what it was told. We had made another friend!

CHAPTER 7

AND THEN THERE WERE FOUR

The arrival of Billy Mathewson in January 1937 increased our numbers to four. Later in the year Edward Hunter from Perth and John Dickins from Pinner, Middlesex, joined us. I remember that Edward had a friend in the Royal Air Force who used to fly up to Pitlochry from his training base. I do not know whether he gave us a display of aerobatics but I do remember standing on the balcony leading off the library watching the plane fly past, the pilot waving as he did so. This recognition gave Edward immense prestige and we were proud to know that he was one of us.

It was not long before our numbers were again augmented by the arrival of Michael Anderson, Don Davidson, Tom Stevenson and Peter MacLellan. The latter held the distinction of being the only boy to wear an Eton suit on Sundays. Peter was a leader and became a tower of strength in many school activities – particularly in Scouting. We were not surprised when he, later, became a housemaster at Strathallan and in due course Headmaster of Rannoch School.

One of the events of the year was the annual Rat Hunt. I am glad to be able to assure everyone that this did not take place around the school buildings but at the farm, where Farmer Crawford reigned supreme. What he required was a dozen of our boys who were not too squeamish. They were armed with stout sticks and told to space themselves around the stacks which were to be taken down. As the rats emerged from cover, they were quickly dispatched by the crudest of methods. The slaughter was horrendous, though the chance of escape was fairly high, depending on the skill of the executioners. I wonder what the boys had to say when they wrote home – I also wonder what the parents thought about the type of agricultural education we were giving their sons! However, we were doing the farmer a good turn by helping him to get rid of vermin which, incidentally, might have found its way down to the school. That, at any rate, was how we tried to justify our involvement in the massacre, but how many boys would have been removed from Croftinloan had any of the more sensitive parents seen the operation I do not know. I think some parents would have been more alarmed to know that Farmer

Crawford kept a large Ayrshire bull which he was not always able to confine. When walking up to the farm one day, I came face to face with the monster. Fortunately, he did not seem to be interested in me but I was afraid that he might make his way down to the school and cause havoc there. He proved to be more benign than the average Ayrshire bull: to my relief he turned round and went home. I later complained to Mr Crawford about his inadequate fences. He turned on his heel, showed great restraint and, like the bull, returned home!

By January 1939 numbers had risen to fifteen but, more importantly for me, at any rate, I became engaged to Muire Murray-Lyon. Her parents (Major-General and Mrs D. M. Murray-Lyon) lived in Pitlochry. In those days, tennis parties were held regularly and, both being very keen on the game, we used to meet at these. We became engaged in February and were married the following August. It was certainly providential that I had found someone who was prepared to tackle the problems which would be caused by the War. It was a daunting task but with the marvellous help given to us by our local suppliers – Mr Martin the grocer, Mr Brown the butcher, Mr Marshall the coal merchant, and others – my wife did a great job in seeing the boys had sufficient to eat. Sadly, she died in 1963 after a long and debilitating illness in which she had been marvellously supported by her doctor, Dr Willie Grant and by her minister, the Rev. John Wright – both of whom had brought her a great deal of comfort.

When I was at my prep school there were two brothers who, unjustly, became very unpopular. Though the First World War was past history, the rumour was circulated that their father had been something rather terrible – a War profiteer! I do not think we knew what that meant, but we were given to understand that it was something pretty disgraceful. If it was, we too, at Croftinloan were guilty of making capital out of the War. I am not suggesting that parents turned up, unannounced, expecting us to accept their boys on the spot but we did become very popular for, perhaps, not the best of reasons. We were in what was called a safe area and the many empty places were filled much more quickly than we had anticipated. By the end of 1940 the minutes at the A.G.M. read: 'It is regretted that a number of parents have had to be informed that there are no vacancies in the school.' By 1941, we were actually making a small profit!

CHAPTER 8

A MISCELLANY

Initially, organised games in the real sense of the term were not possible. We did attempt to play some cricket, though it may not have borne much resemblance to the real thing. In order to get somewhere near the recognised number of players, the teaching staff (two), my sister (whose method of keeping wicket was a little unorthodox) and the under-gardener (Willie Watt) were roped in, willy-nilly. Everyone batted, everyone fielded. Willie had two great assets – a good eye and immense strength. He believed in scoring quickly or getting out quickly and he often succeeded in doing both. Scores could at times be high and it was not unusual for Blair Macnaughton to notch up a century. One boy did not enjoy the game one little bit and resented the fact that it was a compulsory activity. When he was bowled (and that was frequently and early) he had a habit of bursting into tears and refusing to be comforted. The modern tendency in the cricketing world is to knock down one's wicket or to argue with the umpire. Tears are preferable!

None of these early pioneers will ever forget the day Peggy arrived at Croftinloan. Peggy was a Shetland pony which was to give us endless fun and exercise for the next few years. She was gifted to the school by a cousin of mine and, when not saddled for riding, pulled a small Victorian trap behind her. Peggy had decided early in life that man was Enemy Number One and that she was, therefore, going to try to outwit him at every possible turn. The field in which she lived and lazed is to this day called 'Peggy's Field'. Like some of those who sat on her, she was not overfond of work. However, I have to give her full marks for cunning. She would allow us to get very close – with bit and bridle hidden from sight but a handful of oats very visible. Just when we thought we were going to be successful in catching her, she would kick up her heels and be off!

Hew Grant refers to what he calls 'an amusing incident', but I saw it in a different light. When Peggy bolted, pulling the trap after her with the Headmaster in it, I imagine Hew was not the only boy to be amused. Apparently, I was last seen disappearing into a thick clump of bushes. With his tongue in his cheek Hew adds: 'Fortunately, he was none the worse of the humiliating experience'. I do not know whether he reported what I said as I emerged from the undergrowth! I still have a few scores to settle with Peggy, but her death in July 1940 saddened us all, even though she was the most unco-operative animal I have ever met.

I do not think the boys complained of there being too little to do. Apart from a variety of activities which were largely self-organised, they made good use of the tennis-court and putting-green. We climbed the local peaks; went on expeditions; vied with each other as to who could cultivate the best garden or, when increased numbers made it possible, took part in paper chases or treasure hunts.

In those days I was a bit of a fanatic – at least as far as cross-country running was concerned – but it did not take us long to find out that most boys did not share my passion. You might have been surprised (but not if you had known the boys) at the numbers who developed all kinds of physical aches and pains just before a run was due to take place, in order to get Matron to give them a medical line. Matron, however, was not so easily fooled. We tried to cut down the number of 'shirkers' by announcing at the last possible moment that we were going for a run that afternoon. However, the last laugh was not always with me. A boy who had had rheumatic fever earlier in his life (though this had not been recorded in his former medical records and I was thus ignorant of the fact) was constantly lagging behind. As he did not respond to my 'encouragement' this became a little less gentle and I had to shout, as many yards separated us. I am glad to be able to report that the boy survived, but I had been given a fright and was more careful in future.

I am not one of those who believe that young people should never take part in an activity when they are, manifestly, not enjoying it. Nevertheless, his parents may have been a little disturbed to hear, when they read John's Sunday letter, that he had run 'at least ten miles' the previous day and was so stiff that he could hardly walk. In point of fact our runs rarely exceeded three miles. Though we did not bow to the storm and abandon cross-country running altogether, we often sugared the pill by going on paper-chases (except that we used sawdust). Instead of having to run from A to B and back, it was much more interesting to follow a trail, even though it might turn out to be a false one. The boys enjoyed these and the Matron's discrimination was tested less often.

We conquered most of the peaks in the area but never set off without a compass and a whistle, both of which proved to be essential at times. On one occasion, to give ourselves plenty of time, we took tents and pitched them at the base of Schiehallion. It was not surprising that most of the boys were up and about by 6 a.m., as the ground was brick-hard. Three of the eight boys failed to reach the top but they got within sight of it. The leader took only one hour forty minutes to reach the summit. Cold, tired and hungry, we arrived back at school feeling we had achieved something worthwhile.

Perhaps some will remember collecting garnets at Enochdhu (near Kirkmichael), where the competition to find the largest one was very keen. Thereafter, we used to repair to one of the most delightful cottages one could find anywhere. It was at Enochdhu and went by the charming name of The Far End. It belonged to Miss Kirsty Keay and her sister Bunty. No words can express the kindness they showed us for many years. Bunty married Dr Biden, the school doctor, whom we respected and loved, even though he actually laughed when I went down with measles at the advanced age of thirty-two and was feeling very sorry for myself.

We were certainly a small unit but a happy one. I would like to think that I speak for the boys when I say that the more they got to know our lovely surroundings, the more they loved them. Perhaps that would be wishful thinking as far as the majority is concerned, but some were really appreciative of the lovely scenery around them whilst still at Croftinloan. I do believe, however, that beauty has an unconscious effect upon us, only substantially appreciated in retrospect.

Many will remember some of those who were responsible for our 'planned' activities. There was Mr Norman Smart L.R.A.M., who taught music for 35 years or so but for a break during the War. Incidentally, he introduced me to the Beethoven waltzes, for which I am truly thankful. Then there were Miss Sheila Fergusson, the Misses Streather-Booth and Miss Farquhar, who taught dancing during the years I was at Croftinloan. This activity was supposedly a voluntary one, though perhaps too much pressure was exerted at times to make unwilling pupils 'toe the line'. Some, however, actually enjoyed it. Though Hamish Carlton normally derived pleasure from this activity, I do not think he got much enjoyment from the incident which occurred when a team of dancers was invited to give a demonstration at a local hotel. Hamish was invited to show just how the Sword Dance should be performed. As there were no swords available, sticks of bamboo had to be used, held together by elastic bands. All went well for a while but as the heat in the ballroom increased, the elastic bands began to contract and instead of forming the Cross of St George, the bamboo sticks inexorably drew together into a sort of St Andrew's Cross, leaving a vast area in which to dance at one corner and absolutely nothing in the next. Ultimately, the bamboo sticks snapped together and Hamish was left wondering what on earth to do next.

There was one visiting instructor whom we shall never forget. Lloyd Robertson, a local joiner, was in charge of the Carpentry Shop and he made a tremendous impact upon the boys he taught. His enthusiasm and cheerfulness were infectious, as was his humour. I am not sure that the boys understood all he said, however. On entering the Carpentry Shop he would frequently remark: 'Oh, what a stoor!', knowing perfectly well that the boys would require a translation. The high quality of some of the objects produced made us wonder how much help Lloyd had given his pupils. A bird-table, made in those early days by Anthony Service, was still in position in 1971.

When Lloyd died, comparatively young, there was great sadness in Pitlochry and at Croftinloan. His Christian influence had been considerable and he was not one to shrink from expressing his faith in the most natural and spontaneous of ways – often in song. He was given the task of erecting the classrooms, built just after the War. As he hammered in the nails, we were both amused and impressed to hear him singing: 'Onward, Christian soldiers'.

It was during the first term of the school that Nell arrived. She was a Gordon setter and I bought her from Mrs Fergusson of Baledmund. Nell was a really fine and lovely dog and became very popular with the boys. She seemed to possess many of the qualities that poor Peggy lacked. The following year, we welcomed a Shetland collie to which we gave the rather unusual name of Tony. He was equally popular with the boys.

A branch of the Scottish S.P.C.A. was formed in Pitlochry, of which Mrs Fergusson became president and I secretary. A junior branch was formed at school and the boys showed a great deal of interest in animal welfare. Lecturers frequently came from headquarters in Edinburgh to speak to the boys. The General Secretary of the Society – Mr Ripley – is well remembered for the interesting way in which he spoke of the work of the Society and suggested how the Junior Branch could help. Over the years, the boys collected a great deal of money when they virtually ran the biannual Flag Day in Pitlochry. On one occasion, an Old Boy (Bobbie Lucas) who had a very, very ancient car, was responsible for collecting much more than normal. He parked his vintage car outside the local Post Office and waited for the curious to appear. When they did, Bobbie made the most of the opportunity and the S.S.P.C.A. profited by his ingenuity. Apart from publicity of this kind, we held a Garden Fête at Croftinloan, opened by the Duchess of Atholl – part of the proceeds going to the S.S.P.C.A. and part to the Fund which was being raised to help those who had suffered from the bombing of Glasgow. On another occasion, we hired the local cinema for the afternoon and showed the film *Black Beauty*. At the end of the film Commander Fergusson presented the Society's award for bravery to a local shepherd who, at great personal risk, rescued some sheep which had fallen over a cliff.

Our first celebration of St Andrew's Day was held in 1936 and became a feature of school life in the autumn. The following year, Mrs Maxwell invited us to Donavourd House, and another year we were the guests of Major Bald of Easthaugh – the house just opposite the main entrance to Croftinloan. 'Do you know, sir', said one of the boys to me, later, 'Major Bald has a burning bush in his garden'. He had indeed and it did appear to burn when a match was put to it. . .

The firework displays on Guy Fawkes' night were always impressive but they became even more so when David Mitchell's father (who I think was Scottish agent for Brock) supplied us with an arsenal of fireworks. We were very grateful to him for this generosity. Edward James was a lover of bonfires and spent a lot of time preparing for the great night. He used to complain that he did not get much help from the boys, but I had the feeling that he was really happier doing the work himself. What really concerned him was the fact that some foolhardy parents would not keep to the rules and would decide to hold their own independent displays. We may have admired their individualism but rockets in the wrong hands can be dangerous and there were, in fact, some near misses. Rarely did I ever see Edward angry but he was furious with those few irresponsible parents who put everyone at risk.

CHAPTER 9

DIRECTED AND MISDIRECTED ACTIVITIES

Anthony Maclaurin speaks with some feeling of what was known as 'The
Slave Trade'. As he was one of the best 'slaves' I ever had, let him speak
for himself. He writes: 'It was the popular thing to assert one's hatred of
this activity but, in fact, the majority rather liked what they were called
upon to do on Saturday mornings, principally. Briefly, it consisted of
keeping the surrounds of the school tidy; collecting up leaves; cutting
down trees or scrub which had become overgrown or were concealing
the view; making an Assault Course, etc., etc.'. He remembers the
morning when he and three small boys presented themselves at the
Headmaster's study to get their duties allocated. Looking thoughtfully
out of the window and leaning back on my chair, I am reported to have
remarked nonchalantly: 'I want the whole valley cleared. I want to see
the River Tummel from my study window'. Anthony and his slavelets
felt quite overwhelmed and, silently, asked themselves the question:
'Has the Headmaster gone mad?' Now, Anthony – almost thirty years
later – asks another question: 'Mr Brown, did you ever see the Tummel
from your study window?' I have to report, regretfully, that I never did!
However, if one went on to the roof of the building one got an excellent
view of the Tummel valley – but that was risking life and limb. My slaves
had failed me in this instance but I forgive them, because the work they
did elsewhere was excellent and I enjoyed working with such a cheerful,
hardworking bunch of prospective landscape gardeners.

   Gardening was an activity in which a certain amount of direction was
given. It was an 'optional extra' that proved to be very popular, the
number of aspiring gardeners usually exceeding the number of embryo
gardens available. The small plots allocated to the boys were, euphemistically, called 'gardens', and it was amazing what some could do with
such a small area. Some boys brought plants from their homes, but the
majority were supplied by Croftinloan gardens.

   Dryden's description of the man who was 'everything by starts and
nothing long' could have been applied to a minority of our gardeners, but
their land-tenure did not last long. If the gentle warning was not heeded,
the garden was handed over to a boy on the waiting-list. The new owner

was not too pleased with what he had inherited but lost no time in transforming it.

Alisdair Cockburn could never understand why it was said that gardening was good for the mind. In spite of his doubts, he went into partnership with a farmer's son and grew potatoes only! This was probably a form of protest.

Anthony Maclaurin had green fingers and during his time at Croftinloan invariably kept the best garden, though he had difficulty in keeping his plot as he would have wished. Rabbits were, certainly, a problem but he, and others, had a more serious one. There was a fat boy who grew a bit of everything but, apparently, never enough to satisfy his insatiable appetite which, Anthony generously said, he was incapable of controlling. He wandered far in search of food – the walled garden being his favourite target. Sometimes, when danger threatened further afield, 'Billy Bunter' had to be content with what Anthony had on offer. Magnanimous as ever, Anthony hopes that this 'bon viveur' has found an answer to his dietary problems.

It is sometimes said that one cannot put old heads on young shoulders. That may be generally true and it is certainly quite wrong to impose tasks upon young people before they are ready to tackle them with at least a modicum of success. However, many a small boy has put an adult to shame by the way he has carried out a difficult task. If one starts at the bottom and works upwards ('learning by stages', one might call the process), one finds that there are many children in every community who know how to co-ordinate hands and brain. The illustrations I am about to give may seem very insubstantial, as perhaps they are, yet I do think that they are 'pointers' and reveal something of the developing character of the boys involved.

John Dickins, aged 13, was a very responsible boy and one day was given permission to use the Atco lawn mower. It was quite a monster, and a temperamental monster at that. It was almost human in its reaction to work – or so I believed. If one tried to start it up it often refused to turn over, but if one crept up to it, stealthily, the chances were that, taken by surprise, it would respond immediately! You may smile at the simple-mindedness of the Headmaster, but as I used to cut the whole of the playing-field for many years I got to know something of the stubbornness of that machine. It must have reached a good old age when we inherited it from the previous owner of Croftinloan. The best of Atcos, it ultimately phased itself out after a lifetime of service.

But to get on with John Dickins and his remarkable feat. He was cutting the top lawn one day and went too near the steep bank leading to the drive – a bank we used to ski down (at least I did). Halfway down, the bank levelled out for a yard or so, giving one a second take-off. John found himself in real difficulties – I expect he would much rather have been on skis than trying to control a very heavy machine. He must have wondered what on earth he was going to do, but had little time for thought; I believe I would have let go my hold and allowed the monster to find its own way downhill, but John was not going to be defeated. By edging the Atco into a sideway position before it had gathered speed he steered the machine to level ground and to safety. John demonstrated something of his sturdy independent character that day. Sadly, he was killed during the War as a result of an accident on board the naval ship in which he was serving.

On another occasion it was the garden-roller that featured, in this rather amusing story. The incident again took place on the top lawn but the sequel was very different from that recounted above. The school prefects had a few special privileges, one of which was to stroll round the grounds for a short while after the 'commoners' were in bed. One evening, two of the prefects thought they would roll the tennis-court. After a while they got bored with this monotonous exercise and decided it would be rather good fun to see how near they could get to the edge of the lawn, without letting the roller topple down the very steep bank. Of course, the inevitable happened. Frantic efforts to control the law of gravity were in vain. The roller hurtled down the slope, arrived at the first section, leapt in the air before proceeding at speed down the final slope and, after crossing the drive, came to rest in a bed of rhododendrons. The noise made by the runaway roller was heard by the boys in their dormitories, and curious, puzzled faces were soon glued to the windows. The actors in the play – Gordon Fraser taking the leading role – could see members of staff emerging, startled, from the Staff Room. Gordon and his accomplice dived for cover, hoping to get back to the house without being seen. Their intention at this stage was to retrieve the roller, but this proved impossible, and they came to the conclusion that they would probably suffer less by making perhaps not a clean breast of the affair but at least a partial confession. After discussion, it was decided that the consequences would be less severe if they made this to Mr James rather than to the Headmaster who was not noted for his leniency. This proved to be an astute move, as the following conversation shows: 'Sir, we were trying to be helpful by rolling the tennis-court.' The response was brief but encouraging: 'Well done!' 'However', Gordon continued, less nervously, 'The roller got out of control and though we tried to stop it, it slipped over the edge and down the bank.' 'Bad luck!' replied Mr James, 'A brave attempt. But where is the roller now?' 'In the rhododendron bushes beside the playing-field.' 'Oh dear! I don't think Mr Brown will be very pleased about that.' He wasn't, but the thought that the prefects would not be likely to put on a second performance seemed to placate him. This incident may not seem to illustrate the point I am trying to make but the task the boys attempted, though it may have got them into trouble, did reveal something of their ingenuity and honesty.

Our aim at Croftinloan was to avoid being over-protective. We were trying to prepare boys for a world in which risks had to be taken. I do not think we ever wholly succeeded in our difficult and perhaps impossible task but, as boys proceeded up the school, we, in common with most other prep schools, gave the senior boys more and more responsibility. Seemingly unimportant things, such as how to use a scythe, or an axe; how to fell a tree; how to render First Aid, etc., were all part of their training. The fact that a boy was not a member of the Scout Troop did not prevent his learning these and other skills, but in my biased opinion there is a camaraderie within a Scout Troop which is not easily generated elsewhere.

CHAPTER 10

WAR CLOUDS GATHER AND BREAK

In 1937 I took a party of boys to Seefeld in Austria for a ski-ing holiday. Perhaps we should have gone to another country as even then there was a 'smell' of war in the air. I cannot say that we who were enjoying our ski-ing were aware of this but Austria was certainly full of Nazis – our instructor from Innsbruck being one. However, though he was constantly shouting 'Bend zee knees', I never heard him say, 'Heil Hitler!'

Dollfuss, Chancellor of Austria, had been assassinated by the Nazis in 1934 and there was general unrest and apprehension everywhere. Hitler invaded the country in February 1938; we felt that we had returned home not a day too soon.

In September 1939 my wife and I were on our honeymoon, but feeling sure that war was about to be declared we came back earlier than intended, just before hostilities began. Some thought that it would be over by Christmas but their optimism was to get a rude shock. Though we in Pitlochry escaped very lightly, when we heard that Italy had allied herself with Germany we realised that the War was going to be prolonged. We had our moments of alarm. One morning, just after midnight, we heard the unmistakable drone of German planes, which were to drop bombs on Loch Fernat, and at Gatehouse – just a mile from Croftinloan. The following day my sister brought back some shrapnel from the nearer site, just to prove that we had not been dreaming. Possibly the crew were simply unloading cargo surplus to requirements.

The next batch of bombs was dropped during the holidays in the hills above the River Tummel. Whether the target was the Hydro-Electric Power Station we shall never know for certain, but the explosion was terrific. We were glad that the boys were away at the time. One bomb which fell on the moor above Croftinloan did not explode and a Bomb Disposal Unit had to come and deal with it. I had been in Perth that day and, thinking of nothing in particular, turned off the A9 to go up the school drive. I had not gone many yards when I had to brake hard (or thought I had to), narrowly missing one of the limes which bordered the drive. The reason for my somewhat irrational behaviour was that not far away, on the Donavourd moor, a bomb had been exploded by the experts and the shock-waves caused by this had a shattering effect on me. I suppose, in time of war, it is unreasonable to expect advance warning of such an event but I must say I hoped it would not be repeated.

In the comparative peace and quiet of Pitlochry we did not often hear the siren but one night in March 1941 it sounded at 10 p.m. and the All-Clear was not sounded until 2 a.m. the following morning. This may, of course, have had something to do with the Air-Raid Warden falling asleep when on duty! Having been an Air-Raid Warden myself for a time I know how difficult it was to keep awake during the night when for hours on end nothing of significance happened.

Two English preparatory schools – West Downs, Winchester, and Wellesley House, Broadstairs – made plans (which were later implemented) to move to Blair Castle, Blair Atholl and to Rannoch Lodge, respectively, for the duration of the War. We enjoyed our contact with the former school, playing cricket with the boys and attending some of the plays written by their Headmaster, Mr K. B. Tindall. We also attended a performance of *A Midsummer Night's Dream*. This will always remain fresh in my memory because of the fact that the play was acted in the lovely grounds of the castle on a beautiful summer's evening. The romantic setting and the good acting made the play come alive.

Unfortunately, because of petrol rationing we were unable to go as far as Rannoch Lodge, nor were the Wellesley House teams able to come to us for matches and other functions. It was somewhat strange that I was not able to meet the Headmaster, John Boyce, until I went to Oxford to attend an I.A.P.S. Conference: I realised then that I had missed a good deal in not having met John earlier.

We were delighted when we heard that the Leys School, Cambridge had decided to come to Pitlochry and that it was to occupy the Atholl Palace Hotel. This large hotel had been occupied by a girls' school from Scarborough during the First World War, so history was almost literally being repeated. Whilst the Leys School was in Pitlochry, the boys and staff did a great deal for the village. In those days, culture in the area was at a rather low ebb. There was a lot of activity as far as Music and Drama were concerned, but the local promoters seemed to be satisfied with the standard that had been reached in what was a small community. However, two members of the Leys Staff were responsible for raising the level considerably, without in any way being patronising. Indeed, they received the full co-operation of the local people. The school's Musical Director (Mr Heywood), assisted by Mr Hughes, wrote a 'musical' jointly, on Noel Coward lines, and it was enormously successful. Then I can remember cycling into Pitlochry with some of the senior boys to attend a performance of *The Importance of Being Earnest*, also produced, I think, by these two talented schoolmasters. Donald Hughes was a contemporary of mine at Cambridge, and I was glad to be one of the first to welcome him when he arrived in Pitlochry. Apart from his other talents, he was an outstandingly good speaker to young people, and I invited him several times to come to Croftinloan to speak at our Sunday evening services. The talk I remember most vividly was the one he gave on 'Spencer', who was, in fact, a sponge which Donald used to produce, rather dramatically, from his pocket. 'Spencer' had been in circulation quite a long time but wherever he went, he raised many laughs and did a great deal of effective work. In September 1946 Donald was appointed Headmaster of Rydal School in North Wales. The last time I met him was in Oxford, where he was one of the speakers at an I.A.P.S. Conference in 1962. Sadly, he died following a car accident in August 1967.

I imagine the Leys School did not find it easy to adapt to a rural setting, but they settled down quickly and seem to have enjoyed the time they spent in Pitlochry. In order to increase the accommodation, most of the single rooms were turned into doubles. The wardrobes were moved into the corridors and it looked very odd to see dozens of these lining and narrowing the passages as far as the eye could see. The hotel had a nine-hole golf course but, as the school required a playing-field, this had to be sacrificed as there was no level ground elsewhere. Nevertheless, it must have been a mammoth task to fill in the bunkers and iron out the bumps. I can remember umpiring a cricket match and having to interpret the rules rather leniently owing to the uneven nature of the pitch.

We had a very happy association with the Leys and were sorry when the time came for the school to return to Cambridge. Several of our boys – Jim MacDowell, Anthony Service, Douglas Boyd, to name three – went on to the Leys when they left Croftinloan.

Fairly recently, quite a number of Leysians who had been evacuated to Pitlochry during the War held a re-union at the hotel. On the Sunday, a special service was held in the West Church where the boys used to gather during their Highland exile, and to which they had presented a lovely Communion Table in memory of the happy days they spent in Pitlochry.

One Scottish preparatory school thought seriously of moving to Perthshire: Craigflower was, perhaps, rather too near the naval base at Rosyth for comfort. The founder of the school, Frank Wailes, was an old family friend whom I had known since my prep school days. He did not come to Pitlochry to discuss the matter but his wife, his elder daughter Betty and his elder son, Dicky (who, sadly, lost his life just before the evacuation of Dunkirk) arrived one day to explore the possibility of temporary amalgamation. I am sure it would have been a very happy *mariage de convenance*, but the practical difficulties prevented this and the matter was not pursued, to our disappointment.

CHAPTER 11

WAR, WEATHER AND WALKIE-TALKIES

While Hitler continued to cause death and destruction throughout Europe we, at Croftinloan, benefited from his insanity. So many enquiries were received from parents that we were quite unable to find room for all. Obviously, more accommodation had to be found, but the problem seemed insoluble. Then we had a brain-wave – at least we like to think so, though with hindsight we wondered why we had not thought of it before.

The ceiling of the school library (the billiard-room when Croftinloan was a private house) was exceptionally high. Immediately above this room was a luggage loft with a very low ceiling. By lowering the library ceiling, we thought it would be possible to turn this loft into a sizeable room which could become a dormitory, able to accommodate eight boys or so. Mr Gow, an excellent joiner from Blair Atholl, was consulted, and reported that it would be perfectly possible to do this. His exact words were: 'Nae bother at a', Mr Brown' – so for £500 we had a fine new dormitory. In later years it was to become a nursery for the expanding Brown family, before reverting to a dormitory once again.

We were now able to take a few more boys, though classroom accommodation was very limited. We tried to rectify this by fitting sliding doors in one of the rooms, but this was never very satisfactory as the sound-proofing was so poor. Polite, and less polite, messages were often exchanged between one classroom and another, asking if the master in charge could get his boys to make less noise. This was a real test of classroom discipline and one in which some members of staff did not gain very high marks. . .

During the War years, when materials were so difficult to obtain, we had been gathering together, piecemeal, timber, window-frames, wood-wool, etc., but were not allowed to build classrooms until 1945. It was a great day when three new rooms were opened, linked to the main building by a covered-in passage. The sliding doors referred to earlier were stored and used when the Assembly Hall was built in 1961, to divide the back from the front stage. But we are running a little ahead of history; let us return to the years 1940–42, a time of tragedy and of some light relief.

The fall of Singapore in February 1942 probably signified little to the boys, but it meant a very great deal to my family and to myself, as my father-in-law was commanding a division in that part of the world. He was fortunate to escape. We were passing through a very turbulent and threatening period of the War, and it seemed as if the elements were conscious of the fact and acted accordingly. January was a particularly cold month. We had the worst snowstorm in living memory, the snow, accompanied by strong winds, finding its way through closed doors and windows. There were nine-foot snowdrifts on the High Drive leading to Moulin, and Bill Bruce and David Lovelock, accompanied by Edward James, set off one day to look for some extra supplies of food. They returned, triumphantly, with six dozen eggs which Mr Mackintyre of Donavourd Farm had given them. The River Tay was frozen over at Logierat (six miles from Pitlochry). During the day we could keep reasonably warm indoors, each boy being required to saw ten logs to that end in his own and the general interest – an unpopular form of exercise but it did help to raise the body temperature. During the night it was difficult to keep warm: we thought we had enough blankets for the needs of a school twice the size of Croftinloan but found this was not so. Nobody suffered badly from this shortage, though we all got heartily sick of the long spell of arctic weather.

We flooded part of the field and made an excellent ice-rink. Edward James got the boys interested in keeping records of rainfall and temperature, and on one occasion 34 degrees of frost were recorded. Records were kept every day and sent to the Met. Office under a scheme set up for schools. 'Peggy's Field' was ideal for toboganing, but 'ideal' was not the word our pony would have used. True, she had a shed where she could shelter, but she gave clear signs that she resented the intrusion of hordes of savages, hurtling in her direction. Perhaps Christopher Kunhardt will remember my lending him an old sledge which I had knocked together in the Carpentry Shop. It looked indestructible, if not handsome, but Christopher wasted no time in showing that, if you try hard enough, almost anything can be destroyed – giving positive proof of this by running into a tree which, of course, should not have been there!

The tobogganers received a great ovation if they succeeded in sledging from the top of the field and into the pond at the bottom – the Matrons were *not* amused! Later in the year there was yet another very heavy fall of snow (the heaviest since 1895, it was said) and tobogganing became impossible. One method of keeping warm had been removed, but some of us went up to the Cuilc – reputed to have been a quarry at one time but now a lochan – where we had some excellent games of ice-hockey.

In October 1940 we were saddened to hear of the death of Mr George Service who, as a governor of the school, had been such a help in the early stages of its development. He had been senior partner in the shipping firm of Prentice, Service and Henderson; Lord Dean of Guild in the city of Glasgow; a leading figure in the city's business circles and an elder and Session clerk of his church. He spent a great deal of time in his Glasgow house, but he loved to get away to Cove, to his house there and to his yacht. We owe a great deal to him for his wisdom and advice and for the tremendous interest he showed in the development of the school.

Though the War and the tragedies associated with it were ever prominent in our thinking – at least in that of the adult members of the school community – there was, from time to time, some light relief, as mentioned earlier. General rejoicing took place, for example, when early morning cold baths were stopped, not because they were considered barbarous but because of a serious water shortage. To those born in a more civilised (?) age it may seem incredible that there was a time when manliness and cold baths were considered as almost synonymous! They were certainly hated and no trick was too low nor excuse too specious to avoid having to plunge into them.

The arrival of Shirley Brown in 1940 on what was then called 'Empire Day' – 24th May – was exceedingly popular, as the boys were given a holiday to celebrate the event. I think this could be classified as 'light relief'! One boy obviously thought so and remarked: 'I wish Mrs Brown would have a baby every term!'

We were proud to be able to do a little to help on the War effort. The Army 'commandeered' the school grounds, and 1,000 men (500 at one time) erected tents, using part of the estate as a base for military manoeuvres which were carried out under General Ritchie. The men belonged to the Cameron Highlanders and the KOSBs, and they and the boys got on famously together. Walkie-talkies were tried out and iron rations sampled, the boys were given rides in the jeeps, Bren-gun carriers and tanks. Our grounds did suffer a little and we had some difficulty in keeping the troops off the cricket square. 'Don't you know there's a war on, Mr Brown?' remonstrated an irate sergeant. I had little control, perforce, over the movements of the tanks. Their weight caused the grass verges beside the drive to bulge, and these have never really recovered.

Though we had made many friends, we were not sorry when 'peace' once more descended on Croftinloan. Some time after the troops had gone, memories were stirred when we kept finding articles left behind. We were not too surprised to find alfresco loos in the grounds, but it *was* surprising to discover field telephones in good working condition, which Edward James cleaned up and made more serviceable.

Alas, there was no peace in the kitchen! Our ex-Army cook had welcomed the troops with open arms and open ovens. He offered to cook their joints and, more or less, left us to get on as best we could – 'Don't you know there's a war on, Mr Brown?' One day I made what I thought was a friendly gambit. 'Good morning, Potts' (not his real name), I said as I entered the kitchen, seething inwardly but determined to keep cool.

Had I known that he was in one of his worst moods I would have kept away. He gave me a steely look and remarked: 'When you address me I expect you to call me *Mr* Potts'. He then went on to tell me that he was fed up with the job. 'It's like casting pearls before swine', he added, perhaps not realising the significance of the accusation. Disregarding his inference I turned to leave, but before I did so he got in a parting shot: 'Before I left my last job I threw all the pots and pans out of the window'. As he had unwittingly quoted Scripture at me, I might have retaliated by informing him that once a prophet called Nehemiah lost control of himself and 'threw all the household furniture out of the chamber', but I resisted the temptation. . .

As for the boys, they got on with their war efforts. These consisted, largely, of 'tatty-howking'. They were not particularly fond of one farmer for whom they worked, as he showed a remarkable unwillingness to pay them, but they had a much better relationship with Crawford of Croftinloan Farm, who not only appreciated the work they did but paid them promptly.

Working in water-logged fields for hours on end was not very pleasurable but other more tolerable methods were found of raising money to help those fighting, or those suffering because of the hostilities. In 1941 a Garden Fête, which was opened by the Duchess of Atholl was held in the grounds of Croftinloan in aid of the Clydeside Fund (Glasgow having been very heavily bombed). Around 600 people attended – or at least bought entrance tickets. As the entrance to the grounds was on a wide front, some close-fisted Scots climbed in 'some other way' and thus escaped having to pay the entrance fee – I hope they spent a great deal of money on the stalls! Though the Fête was very successful, there was one incident that rather depressed me. A friend of mine – Col. Macqueen-Fergusson – had lent me some golf-balls for use in the putting competition. In those days they were very scarce indeed and could almost have been called 'collectors' items', which is precisely what they proved to be! You can imagine my embarrassment when I had to tell Col. Macqueen-Fergusson that his golf-balls had been stolen. Fortunately, he was not the 'peppery' type of Army Officer and was very understanding.

Mr Wallace Peat certainly did his part in making the Fête a success: he was a professional puppeteer, and we benefited very much from his stay with us as a member of Staff. He wrote a play called *Grammar on Parade*, which was performed on the lawn and greatly appreciated. Mr Peat and his wife made all their own puppets and brightened up many evenings for us with their shows. His adaptation of *The Taming of the Shrew* was especially popular. Mr and Mrs Peat were in great demand, giving shows at the Leys School, Glenalmond, Glasgow High School, Craigflower and elsewhere.

On reflection, we rather welcomed the hard winter of 1941, when the boys' trunks had to be dumped at the bottom of the drive and brought up to school on toboggans – but not for that reason: we gladly accepted the arctic conditions because Senator Knox of the USA had informed the world that Hitler would not carry out his invasion until the weather improved! He even went further and prophesied that, after weather conditions had improved, Hitler would invade in from 60 to 90 days. Just after this pronouncement we had a deluge, accompanied by thunder and lightning. A thunderbolt struck the ground near the changing-room, all lights on phase B glowed faintly, the fences in one of the fields above the school became 'live' because of a fault in the system, a new switchboard was completely burnt out and the barometer read 27.9 degrees. We were ready for Hitler, but actually it was Hess who arrived! According to Quentin Reynolds (the broadcaster with the gravelly voice) who, along with J. B. Priestley, inspired us in their postscripts after the News, Hess had not come to bring peace proposals but to see humanity... I cannot resist quoting Quentin Reynolds' almost immortal words when, with reference to the day on which Germany attacked Russia in June 1941 without any advance warning, he told the story of the hunter who remarked pointedly: 'I've got the bear but he won't let me go'.

It became increasingly difficult to run a school in time of war. My sister – our Matron – informed me one day that she had been called up as a V.A.D. and was to go to a house near Comrie for training. This bad news was to be followed by more, when Stuart Dewar joined the R.A.F. to serve in India. However, we were relieved to hear that Edward James would not have to leave us. Most young schoolmasters were in the Forces and it became almost impossible to find suitable replacements. We were fortunate in securing the services of Mr George Smith. Though a Scot he was, in fact, an American citizen. He proved to be a loyal, hard-working member of staff. I do not know how many Sports Days he attended after leaving Croftinloan, but if he ever missed one we became rather anxious, thinking he might be ill. He ultimately became Headmaster of the Junior Section of the Royal High School, Edinburgh.

Quite a number of those who applied for posts were in their sixties – one even in his seventies. I did have an application from a young man who came from London for an interview. In course of conversation it turned out that he was a Conscientious Objector, but that only came to light after I had asked him why he did not get a job nearer his home. I told him I respected his views but did not respect him for having concealed the truth from me before coming so far. Apparently, the tribunal before which he had appeared had told him that he would be excused military service if he got a post in a school. 'And if you do not?' I asked. 'I shall have to work in a piggery', he replied. I felt it difficult not to smile, but I was genuinely sorry for him.

I received a letter from another applicant, informing me that he had a pleasant personality and adding that his hobbies included stamp-collecting and looking at people. We did not proceed further!

Who would have thought that one day we would have Italian prisoners of war at Croftinloan! They were in a camp at Blair Atholl; one of them was a hairdresser in civilian life and came from Siena. Initially, the boys were rather afraid of him when he came to cut their hair – they may have thought he was going to cut their throats. However, he proved to be a charming little Italian and he speedily laid their fears to rest. Other prisoners were builders by trade and were employed by us to demolish the bank at the back of the main building and then to construct a wall. They were skilled masons and the retaining wall they built, running parallel to our very first classrooms, looks as sound as when they finished it in 1942. I believe they were paid one shilling an hour!

CHAPTER 12

'WHAT DID YOU DO IN THE GREAT WAR, DADDY?'

Perhaps there are some who can remember the posters which appeared
in connection with a recruiting campaign during the First World War.
This question, asked by a small boy, appeared on them and I suppose it
was meant to shame Daddy if he had not yet offered his services to his
country.

When war was declared in 1914 I was only six years old and thus was
unable to 'join up'. However in 1939 I could not excuse myself on the
grounds of age. Alas, the nearest I ever got to the battle front was when a
conscientious recruiting office phoned me up one day and ordered me –
rather peremptorily, I thought – to attend for a medical examination the
following day in Dundee. I thought hard (and probably swallowed hard)
and then replied that I was quite willing to be examined, but suggested
that, possibly, a mistake had been made, as I was the Headmaster of a
boys' boarding-school in Pitlochry and had been informed that I was in a
reserved occupation. There was a long silence, a rustling of papers, a
clearing of the throat, a slight stutter and then: 'I am sorry, sir. We have
made a mistake.' Though I breathed again, I must say that by not serving
in the Forces I felt I had missed out on something – especially after the
War had ended and I was in the company of those who had, when I felt
rather guilty, especially as so many of my friends had been killed or made
prisoners of war. However, I decided that I must do my little bit, and so
took on the job of manning a telephone at the Pitlochry Institute (now the
offices of J. H. Mitchell W.S.). This was unbelievably boring – only once
did German planes pass overhead when I was on duty. I decided to find
employment elsewhere, and was eventually sworn in as a Special
Constable. Life now began to take on a new meaning. My duties involved
patrolling the roads of Ballinluig, in full regalia (complete with whistle). It
was not particularly exciting but at least I was on the move, accompanied
by Peter Campbell, the local blacksmith. We got some exercise together,
tramping the roads and finding a way of using up our 13/-a week boot
allowance.

We had some good fun together, Peter and I, and many a laugh. We
welcomed the rare opportunity of striking the fear of death into the

daring cyclists whose lights were either too bright or non-existent. We were taken very seriously and have to confess that we took sadistic pleasure in the discomfiture of the law-breakers. One night the boot was on the other foot, so to speak: I was quite glad Peter was not with me when the following incident occurred. Returning from my patrolling duties at Ballinluig, I was challenged by a KOSB corporal at the school gates. (I should explain that he and 499 of his mates were carrying out manoeuvres in the grounds of Croftinloan and he was, presumably, told to guard the entrance to the school.) He stared at me, rather suspiciously I thought (even though I was in Police uniform – or because of that fact), and asked me to produce my Identity Card. Luckily, I had SS/JV/69/35 with me, so I was allowed to proceed. On another occasion (although it would have made a better story had the two incidents occurred simultaneously) the lights of my car fused just as I was leaving Ballinluig (about four miles from Croftinloan). I did not think I would be able to keep my job if I were discovered driving without lights, waving a torch madly as I proceeded along the A9, but I was lucky: the entrance to the school had been left unguarded.

For a while Peter Campbell had the whole field to himself, as I went down with measles. I would have been of little use to him, for I became very delirious and could not carry on a coherent conversation. When my wife asked me if I would like her to stay with me in the bedroom, I replied: 'No. Why should I?'

I enjoyed my spell in the Special Constabulary. The training given was interesting and practical, though, fortunately, those of us who were 'Specials' did not require to put much of it into practice. I still smile when I think that I who failed to pass the requirements of Certificate A when at my Public School was promoted Sergeant! I must have matured.

CHAPTER 13

GOOD NEWS

In the early days of the War good news was very scarce. We had to wait
some years for it, and it was very sweet when it came. Some had thought
it would be a short war, but it was not until 1943 that we had much cause
for celebration. The successful outcome of the campaign in North Africa
permitted us to toll the school bell once more. It could be heard in
Pitlochry – two miles away – and it was marvellous to listen to it giving
tongue again.

The night before D-Day those who were still awake could hear a
constant hum of vehicles passing the school gates. They were travelling
along the A9, making for the Channel ports. The gathering together of
such heavy equipment was, I suppose, a very hush-hush operation, but
the noise these vehicles made could not be disguised. It brought relief
and joy to the hearts of those who heard it. Between Le Havre and
Cherbourg airborne troops had already been established. That evening
the King broadcast to the nation and emphasised the need for prayer.
Though Churchill was criticised for going to Normandy (where he was
photographed sitting in a jeep with the inevitable cigar in his mouth) no
criticism seems to have been directed at the King, for some reason or
other, when he visited Advance Headquarters. A good many casualties
were inflicted by the German Airforce, which used pilotless planes for
the first time.

David Hutton and Gavin Crawford arrived at Croftinloan in May 1945,
just in time to celebrate the unconditional surrender of Germany on
the ninth anniversary of the school, which had grown to 45 boys. One
of the first actions after the news came through was to run up the Red
Ensign on our brand-new flagpole, which had been erected in front
of the school. I am not quite sure why we ran up the Red Duster rather
than the Union Jack, but it was probably because we had recently
joined the British Ship Adoption Society and in view of the magnificent part the Royal and Merchant Navies played in the War we wanted to
pay tribute to them. Incidentally, it became the practice for the Union
Jack to be flown on the occasion of a birthday, and if one of the senior
boys forgot to attend to this he was quickly reminded of his duties. I

believe that Peter Bourne and John Dewar were the first to profit by this innovation.

Perhaps I could add a few lines about the B.S.A.S. The fact that we had joined this Society injected life into the Geography lessons (or perhaps I should say 'more life'), as the movements of 'our ship' were followed across the world. Sadly, a number were sunk during the War, but the *Sir William Hardy* remained afloat and we went up to Aberdeen to meet the crew. Some of the members wrote very interesting letters to the boys but though the latter sent replies every time letters were received, the seamen did not correspond very regularly. One cannot expect a busy seaman to be a frequent letter-writer!

It took a long time for the nation to get back to normal. Rationing remained in force for a long time – indeed, some commodities were more difficult to obtain than during the years of war but scarcity was easier to bear. We knew that we would not now come under Nazi domination and thanked God for those who had made it possible for us to remain free. There had, of course, to be a celebration. A whole holiday was announced. The seniors cycled to the Queen's View and the juniors had a picnic – not wildly exciting, you might say, but we had not yet reached the era when many children expect to be entertained most of the time. The boys thoroughly enjoyed what had been arranged for them. In the evening, the 'famous victory' was commemorated by what was described by one Old Boy as one of the best meals he ever had at Croftinloan. Every boy was presented with a parchment from the King, on which was written a message in his own handwriting. I wonder how many still possess this memento of the past.

You will remember that in the very early days of the school we fortified ourselves by recalling the words of the school motto – *J'ai bonne espérance*. By 1950 numbers had risen to 55 and we had no vacancies for four years ahead. Though, I think, we were still the smallest preparatory school in Scotland, we felt that, if we had not scaled the mountain, we could see the summit.

CHAPTER 14

CROFTINLOAN FARM

It was in 1942 that we decided that the Farm buildings needed to be modernised. A milking plant, automatic drinking-bowls and a refrigeration plant were installed. Everything was done to conform to modern dairy practice. We did stop short, however, of providing the cows with sweet music to improve their yield!

Those were the days of the tenant farmer – John Peock being the last. He was a dairyman and had a milk-round in Pitlochry. Obviously, he required much more water for his herd than did his predecessors, who went in for mixed farming. Consequently, difficulties were encountered in dry spells of weather, but John was philosophical about shortages and managed to surmount them.

When Mr and Mrs Peock left, it was decided that we would have a go at running the Farm ourselves. Perhaps we were rather naïve in thinking that it was a viable proposition to run a 100-acre farm profitably, employing, as we did, a manager and his wife full-time. We were even more naïve when we bought a pedigree herd of Galloways in the expectation that local farmers would buy their calves. Eventually, we had to admit defeat, though we tried to delay its impact by buying a white Shorthorn bull at the Perth Sales. We paid £210 for Barslow Silver Jackpot, but although he did his best (with a surname like that he should have done better) we were faced with big losses and decided to capitulate. I had been a 'farmer' for five years and had lost something in the region of £5,000 – this in spite of the fact that Mr Irving Bruges, a farmer himself, who had two boys at Croftinloan, gave most valuable advice. No-one was to blame for the mistaken idea of introducing a Galloway herd into a Perthshire farm – certainly not Mr and Mrs Smith, who were our first managers, nor the indefatigable Mr and Mrs Gibb who followed them.

We were disappointed at the turn events had taken. The boys who worked on the Farm thoroughly enjoyed themselves – at least they looked as if they did. Some of them became very proficient, and when the managers were on holiday they helped with the running of the Farm. No animals died and, indeed, when the managers returned they were loud in their praise of the relief-farmers.

One of the compensations that accrued from the closure of the Farm was that we were suddenly presented with some buildings of which we were able to make good use. The managers' house became a Staff house; the dairy was adapted to make a room for our handyman; the ploughman's cottage provided badly needed accommodation for domestic staff; and the byre became a Shooting Range.

Though work on the Farm was no longer possible (we rented the fields to a neighbouring farmer), we still took an interest in farming. A Young Farmers' Club had been formed earlier. Perhaps boys would have thought twice about becoming paid-up members had they realised at the time that the weeding of potato drills or the thinning of turnips was to be their first job!

An annual pilgrimage was made to the Royal Agricultural Show. In those days the Show was held in a different place each year and we enjoyed visiting the chosen venues. Now that it is held on the same site every year it must make life very much easier for the organisers, but perhaps not quite so interesting to those of a more adventurous nature. What made these shows particularly enjoyable was the fact that from time to time some of the parents of Croftinloan boys, or their friends, had animals entered, and if any of them won an award there was great excitement.

I very much regret not having taken more photographs of the boys at work and of the Galloways and the Ayrshire bull, but I have a good photo of Peter Dunlop, Roger Brown, Calum Michie, Tony Wedgwood and Andrew Henderson attending to two cross calves in the courtyard. This serves as a memento of some very happy days when we all learnt a good deal of what really goes on in a farm. I was not persuaded, however, that I would prefer to work with animals rather than children though, frankly, there were times when I held a different view!

CHAPTER 15

RIDING

I had always hoped to be able to include riding lessons in the curriculum, as I myself was never happier than when sitting astride a horse. We were fortunate in having excellent stables at Croftinloan, but, as they had not been used for many years, some work had to be done on them to bring them up to standard.

Betty, Pepper and Rusty normally lived in Kent, but in May 1940 their owners, Mr and Mrs O'Brien, whose boy, Ivan, was at Croftinloan, asked us to give their ponies temporary accommodation. We were delighted to do so, and I well remember the morning when I went to the local station to meet them. They had been despatched from London by the night train and, as they had been cooped up all night, they were not at all easy to handle once we succeeded in getting them down the ramp. I fearfully mounted the largest (Betty, I think); Mr Cochrane, a local butcher, rode Pepper (with an eye to business?) and although I am not quite sure who piloted Rusty along the A9 at a very early hour in the morning, I think it was Ian Miller. The ride could not possibly have been described as 'comfortable', but at least we reached our destination without accident. The horses were very confused and, naturally, wanted to stretch their legs. We, on the other hand, were determined that they would not be allowed to do so. I thought of John Gilpin but not with any comfort...

Hamish Carlton says that when he came to Croftinloan he was amazed at the breadth of activity available. His admiration, however, did not extend to riding. He had opted to take lessons, but it was not long before he bitterly regretted his decision. He is not likely to forget a pony called 'Step Lightly'. This was, he says, a complete misnomer as the pony was dangerous at both ends and uncomfortable in the middle. During a sudden thunderstorm, 'Step Lightly' was galvanised into equally sudden activity, took off and thundered across the playing-field, eventually throwing the unhappy rider with the greatest contempt. Hamish attributes his fear of horses to that incident in particular, though there were others. However, he has not become a nervous wreck as a result, and in fact is today a very competent consultant and a director of several companies.

Many other ponies and horses followed – Tony, Jumbo, Mousy and Princess – to mention a few. One whose name I have forgotten was a very fine cob and my favourite. One day, however, it let me down badly: I was standing at the front door of the school, holding its reins, when suddenly one of the ponies, in the field not far away, neighed. The cob reared and threw me flat on my back; I was too dazed to notice how many had witnessed my humiliation.

We had some outstandingly good instructors – notably Mrs Margaret Stewart and Miss Catlow. We were indebted to them and to Mr Cormack, one of the parents, who gave us expert advice on the selection of ponies suitable for beginners. Only once did he make a mistake. He bought a delightful little pony for us, but its high spirits made it unsuitable if not dangerous. I seemed to be the only one who could ride it, though it was too small for me. It was exchanged for a less fiery mount.

Riding was very popular with the boys. About thirty took lessons, and these could not be fitted into the time allotted for games and other activities. Thus, when a boy should have been in the classroom, he might find himself, to his delight, on the back of a horse. Requests such as: 'May Michael Anderson go for his riding lesson, sir?' were not popular with masters, not surprisingly. Nevertheless, we do not regret having introduced this activity into the school curriculum, as there were quite a number of boys who did not shine at traditional games such as Cricket, Rugby, Tennis or Hockey but who derived enormous benefit both from learning to control a pony and from looking after their mounts in the stable.

There came a time when the responsibility of engaging riding instructors, buying in feed, selecting suitable ponies, and attending to the financial side of the venture became too much for us. We therefore approached Capt. Milton of the Bridge of Earn Riding School and asked for his help in attending to most of the matters listed above. We still looked after the ponies in our stables, but this arrangement did not work out well, principally because of the big increase in feeding costs; we did not feel this could be passed on to the parents, and so riding had to be discontinued. It was our hope that some would continue to ride when they left us, though we scarcely expected this hope to be realised in the case of the rider of 'Step Lightly', for whom riding was a nightmare.

When the time came for the ponies to leave there were literally tears in our eyes. It was flattering that those which had been with us during the War did not appear to want to leave Croftinloan. Rusty was determined not to enter the horse box, Betty broke her halter and Pepper was very obstreperous.

CHAPTER 16

'E.M.J.'

It would be impossible to write about each and every one of the many first-class members of the Staff who were at Croftinloan from 1936 to 1971. There are a number, however, who because of their dedicated and often lengthy service have earned a special place in these memoirs.

When the doors opened for business on 7th May 1936 there were only two members of the resident teaching Staff – Tom Kirkwood and myself. He was an excellent schoolmaster and during his short stay impressed us with his efficiency and his understanding of boys. Tom was followed by Stuart Dewar, who was an all-rounder. A lover of music and literature, a good cricketer and generally involved in everything which interests a boy, he helped enormously to strengthen the foundations of the new school.

There were two schoolmasters, however, who spent most of their lives at Croftinloan, and I would like to write more fully about each of them. We shall always be indebted to Stuart Dewar for the part he played in persuading Edward James to join us. After taking a Natural Science degree at Cambridge and gaining teaching experience in an English preparatory school, he came to Pitlochry in 1939.

Edward, in my view, approximated very closely to what I think makes the ideal schoolmaster. He never talked down to the children, nor did he make the mistake of treating them as adults. Whether teaching Science, Maths or Scripture, he set himself very high standards: at an inspection carried out by H.M. Inspectors, his teaching was singled out as quite outstanding.

Music, Ornithology, Botany, Science and Photography were Edward's main interests, and he shared his knowledge with the boys. When my wife and I retired in 1971 and went to live six miles south of Pitlochry, he asked me to let him know if, and when, I spotted any unusual birds. One day I was thrilled to see a number of waxwings perched on a *viburnum opulus* in our garden. I phoned Edward immediately and told him that he had better come out at once as, otherwise, the birds would have gone. 'No hurry!' replied Edward, 'If they have just arrived, they will be with you for quite a while.' He was right: when he arrived with some keen young ornithologists, the birds were still enjoying the berries on the viburnum. Edward knew how to make haste slowly. On another occasion, he approached me looking rather concerned. When I asked him what was wrong, he informed me that there was a serious shortage of frogs throughout the country. He then asked me if I would put some Croftinloan frog-spawn into my garden pond to help to increase the population. I agreed, and our garden was later populated by a horde of slimy amphibians.

As Housemaster of Ballyoukan Lodge, Edward had every opportunity of observing 'all creatures great and small' (at least, the latter). Ballyoukan Lodge was one of the oldest houses in Perthshire and 'long-legged beasties and things that go bump in the night' had been breeding there for centuries. Provided they did not exceed bounds, Edward kept on excellent terms with them. However, his interest was not only local. I well remember his trying to keep a praying mantis alive. This was, of course, not a product of Ballyoukan, but a present from a Pitlochry doctor on his return from a holiday in Provence. I believe the praying mantis came from the island of Hyères – south of Toulon. Alas, the P.M. did not like our climate and died.

Many have written to express their gratitude to E.M.J. (or 'Sid' as he was often called) for all that he did for them. Jeremy Moon (now an Army Officer) was one of his admirers, referring to him as a wonderful companion, example and teacher. Long after Jeremy had left Croftinloan, Edward kept in touch with him and helped him with many of his difficulties. I treasure a letter I received from Richard Yarrow, some time before his death in 1987, in which he writes of Edward's strong faith and of its infectious nature. On Sunday afternoons a small group would meet at Bally for Bible study: this was no academic exercise but something very practical, and the teaching they received had a lasting influence on many. Richard, for example, became director of a Christian Outdoor Centre at Nethy Bridge. Though he died as a young man, he passed on to many something of the faith he had received.

Nick Bawtree, now a prep school headmaster, states that it was Edward James who quietly opened up for him the meaning of the Christian way of life, and says he was impressed and fascinated by the illustrated talks Edward gave at our Sunday evening services – *Things that are apt to go wrong, Road Signs, The Rooms of a House*, to name but three.

These talks gripped the boys, but it was the man behind the message, and the unembarrassed way in which he spoke, that impressed us all. It was crystal clear that he lived out his faith. Children are often much more perceptive than they are given credit for and can detect anything spurious or inconsistent. I do not suppose they could have put their thoughts into words at the time, but from the letters received from them as adults it is clear that Edward had a profound influence on those who looked upon him more as a friend than a schoolmaster. One O.C. reports that before he went to Merchiston Edward gave him a copy of *Daily Light* (which includes nothing but verses from the Bible). The writer goes on to say that he rather drifted away from the Church, but returned because a basic faith had been built into his make-up; *Daily Light* lives at his bedside and is one of his most treasured possessions. Another example of Edward's concern for the boys after they had left Croftinloan is illustrated by the fact that before David Urquhart went to Rugby (where, incidentally, he became Head Boy) Edward wrote to a friend of his on the Staff and asked him to make himself known to David, which he did. Yet another O.C. writes to say he thanks God his path and that of E.M.J. crossed at Croftinloan.

On the 'lighter' side of school life, Nick refers to the fact that he frequently suffered at the hands of 'Jammy' (another 'sobriquet'). One night, he and his accomplice were caught chasing each other round their dormitory after Lights Out, to muted encouragement from the onlookers. The two offenders were marched up to Jammy's study and given an opportunity of defending themselves. Apparently, their defence broke down and they prepared themselves for the worst. 'Which one first, sir?' they asked, simultaneously. 'There's room for two', replied the executioner. So, had you been able to look in, you would have seen two rather unhappy schoolboys bending over a chair. Nick recalls that it was the worst beating he had ever had, not because of its severity (E.M.J. never overdid this) but because neither of the miscreants knew on whom the first, or subsequent, strokes would fall, or indeed when the punishment would be completed. There was never any feeling of resentment, because Edward was always strictly just and fair. For some while afterwards 'Room for two' became quite a jest between the executioner and the executed. Just occasionally, the unruly found themselves at the end of the notorious hairbrush; on more than one occasion it was 'lost' and a slipper had to be substituted. Though corporal punishment has come in for a lot of condemnation lately it was considered, in those 'unenlightened' times, that there was a good deal of merit in the 'quick, short, shock'. Jeremy Moon, on the receiving end, thought so. He asks the question, 'Who says that corporal punishment is ineffective?' and then proceeds to answer it: he had lied to E.M.J. and received what he considered his just reward. Jeremy adds, 'I don't think I have told a lie since that day', but after a moment's reflection remarks, honest as ever, 'at least not a lie as big as that one'!

Some of those who thought they could trade on E.M.J's good nature found out that he was not that easily fooled. Once he drew attention to a lot of ink blotches on the cover of an exercise book belonging to Jeremy Bruce-Watt. Jeremy tried to defend himself by saying: 'Oh, those were made last term, sir'. On looking more closely, Edward discovered that the ink was still wet. Jeremy's defence crumbled. As, however, both master and pupil shared a passion for butterfly collecting, possibly Jeremy was let off fairly lightly. . .

Ballyoukan was reputed not only to be one of the oldest houses in Perthshire, but, as Rob Brown recalls, one of the coldest. Edward was well aware of this and turned a blind eye when the Matron supplied the half-frozen boys with hot-water bottles, following up this act of thoughtfulness with hot chocolate drinks on Saturdays, or 'more often if the need justified it', Rob adds. Edward, not to be outdone, now and again treated his charges to strawberries and cream during the summer term. The boys who went to Ballyoukan were specially selected and, though some had lapses from time to time, most of them deserved the privileges they received.

Edward's life would have been incomplete had he not married Jean. She completely shared Edward's interests and made a marvellous housemaster's wife. It is difficult to write about her without appearing to be fulsome, but her contribution to Croftinloan was so great that it would be well-nigh impossible to exaggerate it. Like her husband, she had a close rapport with the boys – they loved her and she them. Whether in class teaching, archery, speaking at our services or indulging in 'small-talk', her charming personality was evident. Jean died in 1976 when on holiday in Wales with Edward, filling us all with a great sense of loss and sadness, but with thankfulness to God for having sent her to Croftinloan. Edward was, of course, sustained by his faith, but he must have been a lonely man without her, though he was not the type to show it. When he, himself, became ill, we admired him for his courage and humour. He carried on working even when he was really very ill indeed, but died at his brother's house in Surrey, on 10th March 1980. I was glad to be able to attend the memorial service and, since Edward was a loyal and dependable friend, steady as a rock, I found the experience very moving but would not have wanted to miss it.

CHAPTER 17

'R.F.L.'

I will not disguise the fact that I tried for many years to get Rupert Lanchester to join me at Croftinloan, as he had become a very close friend from our days together at Ardvreck and was a first-class schoolmaster. We seemed to speak the same language and, largely, to have the same thoughts about the running of a preparatory school. However, he was very happy at Ardvreck under the Headmaster, David Smythe, and his work there was greatly appreciated. So why should he leave and join someone who had started something which might succeed or, conceivably, fail? I ceased to press the matter, believing that one day I would hear from him that he would like to join us, if the offer was still open. This turned out as I had hoped and, to my great delight, he arrived at Croftinloan in 1948. I can assure you that the red carpet was laid out for him!

Rupert was a man of many parts and many nicknames. His commitment to Scouting (described in Chapter 21) might have seemed to an onlooker to be almost a full-time activity, but he had many other interests. He played chess with the boys; collected stamps – particularly Russian ones (for which he was labelled a Communist); set the annual General Knowledge paper; completed the *Times* crossword puzzle (in red ink!); took a great deal of interest in Athletics, and organised the Swimming Sports. He spent many hours hand-picking the weeds which grew around the Long Jump pit and on the steps leading up to the school from the playing-field. I suggested that it might be quicker if he used weed-killer, whereupon he gave me a look of polite scorn, for he believed in the therapeutic value of his method. Rupert also played an important role as the school Banker. Anthony MacLaurin mentions the fact that he taught him how to account for money. Every term, the pocket-money brought back to school had to be handed over to R.F.L. for safe keeping. (Latterly, this normally amounted to around £2.) Each boy was given a bank book and it was made quite clear that money could only be withdrawn when every penny had been accounted for. Anthony adds that this was a bit irksome but that he is now very grateful for the discipline involved. Perhaps this helped him to become the successful businessman he is today!

Though Rupert's nicknames did not exceed his interests, he had quite a number. 'Lanky' (or 'Lanch') explain themselves, but no-one seems to be quite sure of the origin of 'Cruise'. There was a rumour that he had been born on board ship, off Cape Horn, when his parents were on a cruise, but as that could not be verified we had to look elsewhere for an explanation. Richard Yarrow suggested that R.F.L. was called 'Cruise' because of his nightly habit of 'cruising' round the dormitories after Lights Out, with what he intended as a stealthy tread but which sometimes alerted the boys in dormitory IV just as some of them were preparing to carry out one of their 'dares'. One of these involved going down the fire-escape, chasing each other around the playing-field (in pyjamas, of course) and getting back to bed without being caught. One boy (who claims fame as a 'rebel'), along with an accomplice, both of whom will eventually be named, recounts this incident. At midnight, when the moon was full – it had to be, as they wanted to savour the enjoyment of taking maximum risks – these two pioneers met in the drying-room and changed into Rugger kit. They walked up the High Drive leading to the village of Moulin (three miles away), down through Pitlochry, back along the banks of the Tummel to the level-crossing below the Main Entrance to the school, up the Drive and so to bed. Jeremy Moon tells me that he and Ronald Gunn only occasionally showed such bravado and asks me if I was aware of their nocturnal expeditions. He is still awaiting an answer!

'Cruise' was very fond of an old raincoat. No-one seems able to remember a time when it wasn't part of him, for its use was not restricted to gardening sessions – it appeared on formal and informal occasions alike. At Hallowe'en the boys had great fun trying to identify disguised members of the Staff in the dark, as they moved around in the grounds. When a disguise was successfully penetrated, the 'Staff-Spotter' was given some sweets. Wattie Barbour remembers an occasion on which he was completely fooled: he came abreast of what he thought was a scarecrow or, possibly, the guy for the bonfire, and passed on. What he had passed by was no scarecrow but R.F.L. wearing his famous coat – no sweets for Wattie!

To match his raincoat, Rupert owned a 1928 Alvis: YX 9047 was a wonderful old car, probably the noisiest on the road – worthy of an entry in the Guinness Book of Records. Long before the car became visible one could hear it staggering up the drive. Those who knew the owner will not be surprised to hear that it was always kept in immaculate condition. One would have expected Rupert to polish the fabric-covered vehicle, but what was unseen – the engine – was also polished till it shone. Incidentally, R.F.L. had a phenomenal memory for numbers. He could tell me the numbers of all the cars I owned over a period of 47 years, whereas I am able to remember the number of his Alvis simply because I made a note of it. An enthusiastic train-spotter in the days of steam, he had plenty of opportunity for exercising his uncanny ability for remembering numbers, although he was no mathematician. He took a Classical degree at Cambridge, teaching Latin, and a little Greek, at Croftinloan.

Though Rupert was able to cope with the idiosyncrasies of his own car, he did not find it so easy to drive a modern car. At one time, I owned a Morris Isis 7-seater Estate car – I have to confess that I cannot remember its number. . . One Saturday, Rupert offered to drive this car to an Away match. What he did not know was that it was rather difficult to put into reverse gear, but one of the passengers – David Greenhalgh, the Head Boy – had learnt the knack. How he learnt this we can only guess! Anyhow, as he was sitting next to R.F.L. he was in a perfect position to give advice should it be required. As long as David was at hand to pass on his expertise, all was well. The driver parked the car in front of the school we were visiting. The boys got out, went off to change into their cricket gear and then proceeded to the field. All would have been well, had not Rupert's consideration exceeded his wisdom. He offered to give the Headmaster a lift to the field, but soon realised that he had taken on a difficult task from which there was no going back. He tried many times to reverse the car but in vain: eventually he had to drive forward over an immaculate lawn in order to get on to the driveway. It would have been interesting to hear what the Headmaster said to R.F.L., and vice versa!

I treasure a book of Rupert's containing the names of all the boys he taught in his long teaching career – at Ardvreck and at Croftinloan – but he had another book which I do not possess. It is distinguished by his neat, immaculate handwriting, and Rupert called it his 'Good Deeds' book. I do not think I ever saw it, but Anthony Maclaurin, who did, told me that it recorded all the requests that had been made to him during his life and that every request was numbered, the last entry being No. 34,000! Rupert was a most unostentatious man and did not keep these records for self-gratification but because he had a tidy, methodical mind which had to be satisfied.

How true it is, as Richard Yarrow wrote, that most memories of school are linked to members of the Staff. Generations of pupils at Ardvreck and Croftinloan looked upon R.F.L. as a friend and he was never more pleased than when Old Boys visited the school, principally to see him. They liked his quiet humour and respected him for his Christian faith. When he died in 1982 we realised we had said au revoir to a man whom Byron would have described as 'a Gentleman from top to toe'.

PLATE 1

Aerial view of the School: 1969 (*Aerofilms Ltd*)

The School Staff outside the main door in 1947: Margaret Marshall,
Hugo Brown, Muire Brown, Stuart Dewar, Edward James, Janet Kerr,
Mark Kidner, Helen Brown.

PLATE 2

The first three boys in 1936:
Blair Macnaughton, Anthony Service,
Robert Buchanan

Frances Berwick on her retirement as
Matron in 1986.

The first seven: drawing breath on their walk to the Birch Park.

PLATE 3

Peggy pulls her weight

Setting off on a ride in the grounds: Mrs Margaret Stewart and two pupils.

PLATE 4

Members of the Young Farmers' Club at work.

John and Willie Watt, our first gardeners, give instructions in tree-felling.

PLATE 5

Rupert Lanchester as time-keeper at Sports Day.

Joe Anderson, the cricket professional, instructing at the nets.

PLATE 6

Aerial view of Ballyoukan Lodge *(Aerofilms Ltd.)*

Bringing home the Yule Log up the school drive.

PLATE 7

Scouts on duty: inspection time at a Camp near Aberfeldy.

Scouts off duty at the Aberfeldy Camp.

PLATE 8

Acting in the production of *Le Poltron Courageux* in 1965.

George Cansdale and Percy the Python.

CHAPTER 18

'MISS B.'

Fourteenth January 1954 was a red-letter day in the life of the school, for it was on that day Miss Berwick arrived at Croftinloan. Initially, she was assistant to the Matron, Miss Macpherson, one of the most efficient and kindly matrons we ever had at Croftinloan. On her retirement, 'Miss B.' (as she was to be affectionately called) became Matron and soon proved herself a worthy successor, forging strong links with the children and their parents. It was significant that when she was asked by a reporter of the *Dundee Courier* what qualities were most needed by a school matron she replied: 'Patience, understanding and a love of children'. She certainly possessed these qualities, but I would add two more – a sense of humour and the ability to get on with others, however *difficile*. She was a great pourer of oil on troubled waters – sorting out the various squabbles and problems which arose from time to time.

The day in the life of a school matron is a long one and often extends into the night. Children would arrive at her bedroom door as if they thought they required a major operation! Their anxieties were often expressed very briefly: 'Miss B., I can't sleep'. Most of us would have been annoyed at being disturbed in the middle of the night, but Miss B. wanted to know the reason for the child's sleeplessness, and her sympathy probably helped to solve the problem. Rob Brown says that no-one ever had a bad word to say of her. On the rare occasions when she got angry, she would later apologise to the one who had incurred her wrath, thereby making a friend for life. Rob adds: 'She knew a thing or two about psychology.'

I do not know whether the Matrons who were at Croftinloan during Anthony MacLaurin's stay there would like to be described as 'a rare breed, some tough, some loving', but he wisely makes no attempt to specify into which class he would put them! He thought it rather daunting for a New Boy to be confronted by a Matron wearing a white starched hat. However, when Miss Berwick succeeded Miss Macpherson the white hat was discarded: whether this was due to pressure exercised by Anthony, I do not know. Miss B. may have looked more informal than her predecessors, but whatever she did she always showed a great deal of concern for, and understanding of, the children under her care. During her time at Croftinloan she had a number of serious illnesses to deal with, and in each case she made parents realise that their children were indeed safe in her hands.

Miss B. knew when to put her foot down, being well aware that a happy school is a disciplined one. However, she had a blind eye – like Nelson, who is reported to have said at the battle of Copenhagen: 'I have only one eye – I have a right to be blind sometimes'. So had Miss B. This 'defect' – an essential requisite of anyone working with young people – prevented her from seeing things that are not all that important, but one blind eye is sufficient! A nameless boy (though not nameless to me) had a book called *What every squirrel knows*, which had been hollowed out and contained bubble-gum. Though confiscated from time to time, it was always returned – to be re-filled. In law, Miss B. could probably have been called an 'accessory' before (and, probably, after) the fact, but she could claim diminished responsibility due to her 'blind' eye!

I wonder which eye she used when boys stuffed scones into the wall outside the changing-room or when they poured their glassfuls of milk down the drain. I remember doing the same thing at my prep school but that does not mean that I recommend it. If you know anything about young people you will not be surprised that Midnight Feasts held at Ballyoukan were not all that popular. Why? They were allowed!

I have always had a high opinion of the reactions of young people. Just before Miss B. left Croftinloan she received a card from one of the pupils. On it was written: 'To Miss B. The best Matron the world has ever seen' – a spontaneous expression of love and gratitude, echoed by many who perhaps could not express themselves so clearly. Miss B. never sought the limelight but she was adept at doing good by stealth. We often heard of her 'little, nameless acts of love' long after they had been performed.

CHAPTER 19

PROXIME ACCESSIT

In his short stay at Croftinloan, from September 1952 to December 1954, Michael Botting made a great impact on everyone. He was the type of man whom headmasters sometimes dream about but rarely meet. If we could have persuaded him to change his mind and enter the teaching profession rather than the Church on a permanent basis we would have tried, but we knew that our efforts would be in vain.

Not everything in the garden was lovely – Michael found the Staff Meetings rather boring! Perhaps he would have found them more bearable if he had realised that the man in the chair sometimes held a similar opinion. However, we gave him little time to be bored: he was asked almost immediately to take charge of various activities and to lend a hand in others. Being very keen on Puppetry and on Handwork of all types, he was given the exclusive use of a room on the top floor of the building where he gave the boys some practical instruction.

It had always been the practice to present an annual play but, in addition, each form was now encouraged to perform one written by its members. If they felt they were unable to do this they could seek advice before selecting a suitable play, but rarely did they require help. Jeremy Moon says that he had a brief spell of glory in the dramatic world when he directed *Alice in Wonderland* and acted in it: the joint role of director and actor seems to have embarrassed him a little but the show was a great success. Sometimes the Staff was anxious lest the rest of the school would not want to attend a not very professional performance and, initially, we tried a little 'persuasion' in order to make quite sure that there would be a sizeable audience, but soon found this quite unnecessary, as most of the school flocked to see these amateur efforts. Boys are not too keen on making fools of themselves in public but they love to watch others doing so!

Michael produced a number of school plays – notably *Emil and the Detectives* (with 13 different scenes, including the inside of a railway carriage). One boy, with a very bad stammer, had quite a big part and spoke his lines without a trace of his impediment. The play was worth performing for that fact alone. Probably the best of Michael's puppet shows were *The Sorcerer's Apprentice* and *David and Goliath*. Edward James, as ever, was behind the scenes helping with the staging and lighting. Those were the days when we were very restricted by lack of space. What had been a laundry and wash-house was converted into a gymnasium (if one can use such a grand term) and, using a moveable stage, plays were produced in this rather small area. On occasions we managed to pack in some 80 people but not with comfort!

There were few activities in which Michael did not participate. He shared the running of the Scout Troop with 'R.F.L.'. I have vivid recollections of him dashing around the grounds umpiring the Wide Games which were so popular with the boys – and obviously thoroughly enjoyed by both the S.M. and the A.S.M. Michael was an enthusiast and whatever was 'on' at the time he was usually involved in it. I admire but do not envy him for being the first member of Staff to dive into the Swimming Pool when it was opened in 1954!

Michael did something in 1953 which did arouse my envy, as I had always longed to do it myself. He was escorting the London party when the train overshot the platform at Pitlochry. The boys were all at the front of the long train and by the time they got down the corridor to a part that opened on to the platform the train was moving out. It was then that Michael acted – pulling the communication cord! The train stopped abruptly. The guard jumped out, demanding an explanation. He did not appear to be too pleased but somehow or other Michael managed to placate him – though it was he who should have apologised for his precipitate action.

Often, when going across to Ballyoukan or returning to school, Michael would be befriended by robins. Perhaps they thought he was St Francis of Assisi! They would perch on the handle of his bicycle (thumbing a lift?) without a trace of fear. Whilst on the subject of birds, I would like to refer to a conversation which Michael overheard one day and which very much amused him. The name of the tenant-farmer at Ballyoukan was Swan and he had some hand-reared pheasants which used to wander down to the Lodge. Someone was trying, unsuccessfully, to convince a newcomer that these birds were swans!

Very reluctantly, we said au revoir to Michael. Fortunately, in the years ahead, we were to see him fairly often as not only did he send his son, David, to Croftinloan but he and his wife, Mary, became so fond of Perthshire and of the Pitlochry Festival Theatre that they frequently came North.

The reminiscences of Miss Roma Stewart make interesting and amusing reading. She had come to Scotland from the South to be nearer her brother, who was Under-Secretary at the Scottish Home Department; we were to benefit from his appointment. When I asked the Headmaster of the school where Miss Stewart had taught, before coming to us in January 1951, if he would be good enough to let me know something of her teaching methods, he replied, laconically, that her methods were all her own! This may have sounded a trifle disparaging, but I am sure it was not intended to be. Anyhow, whether her methods of teaching were her own or not I do not know, but I do know that they were very effective.

One summer term there was a shortage of domestic staff – a frequent occurrence. As there were no Trade Unionists on the Staff, lines of demarcation were not clearly drawn, so, led by Bill Hayward, an Australian and a superb cricketer, with Miss Stewart and Leo Hoskyns bringing up the rear, the trio formed up in military style, heels clicking, and marched towards the changing-room, where they proceeded to clean the basins. Evidently their initial enthusiasm wore off before the task was completed. They decided they had had enough and invited Roma Stewart to accompany them to the river in Bill's car. This proved to be an unfortunate decision and location as, standing in the Tummel, fishing, was the Headmaster who, tactful as ever, pretended not to notice the shirkers.

Roma loved everything colourful and says she was delighted to have been given the run of the garden. She did the flower-arranging in the school, not only on special occasions but on a daily basis, and her classroom was a joy to behold. Her love of everything beautiful was passed on to her pupils, most of whom she says were reasonably well-behaved, though she does name two (I do not) who could be extremely aggravating. She singles out one boy – Aulin Baird – as being a 'true, blithe spirit' and very co-operative and artistic. His promising career was cut short when he lost his life at sea, tragically (see Chapter 26).

One of Miss Stewart's distinctive memories centres round the day on which she passed her Driving Test. She had taken the test in Perth, and to proceed up the South Drive without 'L' plates, cheered to the echo by the boys who lined the route, filled her with a great sense of achievement and pleasure.

Roma was not one to be conveniently (or inconveniently) absent when there was work to be done, and her help on so many occasions was very much appreciated. She took a major part in dressing and making-up the actors for the school plays and in painting the scenery, and particularly remembers 'padding up' Andrew Grimond when he played the part of Bultitude in Anstey's *Vice Versa*. The lounge-suit, borrowed from Edward James, was large enough to accommodate a few cushions!

When Miss Stewart informed us on 11th May 1955 that she would be leaving Croftinloan at the end of the year our spirits sank, as she had contributed so much to the life of the school. Fortunately, we had not seen the last of her, as she returned to us in the autumn term of 1958 to fill a temporary vacancy and remained until the end of 1959.

I feel sure that Rupert Lanchester would have agreed with me in my estimate of Miss Bowie, who came to Croftinloan in January 1940 as Matron. She was Matron at Ardvreck when we both taught there and we had enormous admiration for her, with her many fine qualities – one being her sense of humour. She laughed as loudly as anyone when Rupert presented her with a copy of his parody of the *Lays of Ancient Rome*, featuring Miss Bowie herself. I do wish I could recall the details of her part in the battle 'as she iodined the dead'. Unfortunately, I was never given a copy. She did not mind having her leg pulled. She had been Matron at a well-known girls' school (Highfield) and when she said, for the umpteenth time, 'When I was at Highfield we used to . . .' we delighted in trying to finish the sentence before she had time to do so. Sometimes, however, the boot was on the other foot: on one occasion she asked Hew Grant to go and ask E.M.J. for a copy of yesterday's *Rest and Be Thankful*. He obediently complied but I never heard what effect the request had on Edward or what he said to Hew. . .

Miss Bowie never kept very well, as she had a weak heart, and eventually had to give up her valuable work; she entered a Glasgow Nursing Home in October 1942, where she died in January 1943. She will always be remembered for her kindliness and thoroughness. Parents were most grateful for the efficient way in which she cared for their children.

A number of Old Boys write to say how much they appreciated the good start Miss Gwen Legge gave them in the bottom form – 'my form', as she called it. There was something very personal in her dealings with 'her boys'. No modern 'nonsense' for her. She followed well-regulated lines, believing that the 'Three R's' must have precedence over everything else – and she got results. She did not rule with a rod of iron – she did not need to, as she made her boys feel that she was definitely on their side. Out of school, she ran the Cub Pack and did so efficiently and imaginatively. The Cubs of those days will never forget the wonderful outdoor feasts they helped to prepare – and consume.

Gwen Legge lived with her sister in Pitlochry before going to Leicester, where she died. She had maintained her interest in Croftinloan over many years and used to write the most marvellous letters, almost every sentence of which ended with an exclamation mark!

One of our 'short-stay' assistant masters who left a big impression behind him was Mark Kidner. He came to us just after the War and, amongst other subjects, taught Art. When he left us I believe he went to an Art School in London but, unfortunately, he is now 'beyond our ken'. I wonder if he remembers the disrespectful behaviour of my son Hugh, aged two – he used to go up to Mark and say 'Hullo, Kid'!

Over the years, we were fortunate in being able to appoint some very charming and efficient Junior Mistresses, who were, largely, responsible for teaching the younger boys. I can think of Lila Dickinson, Elizabeth Morris, Carol Fieldhouse, to name a few. Not surprisingly, those mentioned left to get married and we missed them. Robin Laird, an Irish member of Staff, had the effrontery to elope with Carol Fieldhouse, who had done so much for the younger boys and for Music throughout the school, but we applauded Robin for his good taste. Love is said to be blind but not much misses the attention of a small boy – when he is interested. The 'clandestine' meetings of Romeo and Juliet on the playing-field after Lights Out were carefully monitored by the boys of at least one dormitory!

This 'wastage' (as far as the school was concerned) of staff prompted me to write to the Principal of a Teachers' Training College in N. Ireland, where some of these colleens had been trained. I asked her, tongue in cheek, if in future she would do her best to introduce me to Junior Mistresses who were efficient but not quite as attractive as those she had recommended in the past. I think she must have taken me seriously, as an ominous silence followed. I should have known better – aren't all Irish colleens attractive?

CHAPTER 20

GAMES

Some Old Boys have drawn my attention to the fact that our Rugby and Cricket teams seemed to lose quite a number of matches. This is, of course, only reminiscent of the 'Bad Old Days'. Nowadays, the school seems to have developed a capacity for winning matches! In an attempt to defend ourselves, I would point out that for many years we were the smallest preparatory school in Scotland. Nevertheless, we did have some good seasons: when Iain Laughland was Captain of Cricket we won all our matches. As he later captained London Scottish and Scotland for a number of years one might have expected an undefeated Rugby season under his captaincy, but I think this occurred after he had left.

We did have some outstanding O.C. players. Morison Zuill represented Scotland at cricket. Donald Fraser was a most promising scrum-half when at Croftinloan and but for illness I am sure would have represented – or got very near to representing – his country. I remember that after a match against Ardvreck the referee, who was a Scottish trialist, came up to me and said: 'I like the look of your scrum-half. He should go far.' At Merchiston he played for the school and, later, for Ross and Sutherland. His brother, William, was also a fine athlete – one of the most fearless tacklers I have ever met. He played for Edinburgh University and for the Scottish Universities. Had he not emigrated to New Zealand to do research in forestry we would surely have heard more of him in the world of Rugby. Sadly, he lost his life when canoeing on the Derwent, in Tasmania, thirty miles downstream from Hobart, when on an expedition. We think of him as a very fine boy who made friends wherever he went.

We were delighted when a member of the Staff, George Crerar, was appointed President of the S.R.U. As a schoolboy he had played cricket for Scotland and, later, Rugby for the Glasgow Academicals. During his time at Croftinloan he was honoured by being appointed Manager of the Scottish team which went to the Argentine. His wife, Mary, who made an outstanding contribution to the school, was as keen on Rugby as he was and I am sure would have liked to take part in some of the regular school games, if one can judge by the enthusiasm she showed on the touch-line when watching a school match! However, she had to be content with the regular trips she made annually to Murrayfield with George. He became very popular with parents who wanted stand tickets for the International matches at Murrayfield (or unpopular if he could not supply them). He, of course, coached the School Rugby team but there were several other games masters, notably Desmond Bassett and Jimmie Jamieson, who should be mentioned because of their enthusiasm and expertise. George Crerar's death in December 1986 saddened us all. He had done a great deal for the school.

The boys very much enjoyed going to Murrayfield to see the international matches – particularly when Iain Laughland was playing – but, apart from the game itself, it was good to meet quite a number of O.C.s at a pre-arranged spot after the match. When the final whistle blew we usually found we had very little voice left. In 1951 when Scotland beat Wales by 19 points to nil we were exceedingly hoarse! No doubt the boys were overjoyed when it was announced that the Headmaster would be unable to speak at the evening service the following day. . . After one really remarkable match we were not at all hoarse: South Africa had massacred Scotland by 44 points to nil. It was a disastrous match from the Scottish point of view, but once we had got used to the inevitability of defeat we sat back and enjoyed the skills and determination of the South Africans.

Apart from Joe Anderson, who had distinguished himself on many cricket grounds and golf courses and coached our eleven so ably, there were others who did a great deal to raise the standard of the game at Croftinloan. I am thinking of Major Irwin, George Crerar, Bill Hayward and Alan Preen. Bill Hayward was a delightful Australian – and a Cambridge Blue – who came to us, temporarily, because he was said to have strained his back and needed to rest. This injury did not prevent him from coaching and from demonstrating his skills. We were amazed at his hard hitting and at the speed with which the ball took off. He was succeeded by another Australian – Alan Preen – who had come to Scotland, as a professional, to play for Perthshire.

Three cricket matches stand out in my mind. The first was played in 1954 against Ardvreck. We batted first, scoring 17 runs. That, we thought, was the end. Ardvreck, no doubt full of confidence, followed and were all out for 10! The second match was against Lathallan, who had not lost a match that season. I cannot remember the score but Murray Steven was the match-winner, taking 4 wickets for 4 runs. Alistair Tares, however, held the record: when playing against Hurst Grange he took 8 wickets for 36 runs.

Athletics played quite a prominent part in the curriculum. Recognising that not every boy is a natural athlete, we set various standards, the lowest of which could be reached by the near-infirm. Points were awarded and all boys, whether they gained a medal or not, could win points for their House throughout the year. On Sports Day points were awarded for the first six finishers in every final. This was a bit of a headache for the judges but Rupert Lanchester took it all in his stride, probably because he enjoyed it.

Our comparative lack of success in matches was off-set (or so we like to think) by the many activities available to a boy. Though most of them are now commonplace amongst schools, we did seem to be ahead of our time in the variety of pursuits which a boy could take up. With our rather smaller numbers every boy had to participate in organised games, but time was made available for ski-ing, hill-walking, bird-watching, archery, fishing and gardening, apart from other activities already mentioned. Indoors, shooting, billiards, table-tennis, modelling and philately were popular.

CHAPTER 21

SCOUTING

It had always been my intention to start a Scout Troop at Croftinloan. I myself had never been a Scout, either at my prep or Public School, as Troops did not exist at either, but I became a Rover Scout when at Cambridge and very much enjoyed the training I received. When I joined the Staff at Ardvreck School I found there a flourishing Troop, under the leadership of Vernon Chawner, whose whole life seemed to be bound up in Scouting, and I became an Assistant Scoutmaster. Later, Rupert Lanchester, who arrived at Ardvreck a term after me and remained there for seventeen years, became Scoutmaster of the Troop.

One day the Ardvreck Troop was invited to meet the Chief Scout – Sir Robert Baden-Powell, who at the time was staying with the Maxtone Grahams of Cultoquhey, Crieff. We were delighted to accept the invitation, though a little apprehensive. We need not have had any fears as B.P. immediately put us at our ease, asking us to sit down on the grass in a semi-circle whilst he talked to us. He had a certain magnetism about him and the stories he told of his experiences throughout the world enthralled us – we could have listened to him for hours. Many years later I met Lord Somers, the recently elected Chief Scout, when I was attending the I.A.P.S. Conference at Oxford. Like his predecessor, he was an enthusiast and made a deep impression on all who met him. We were very shocked on hearing of his death when he was only 57.

So, very early in the life of the school – before the outbreak of the War – the Croftinloan Troop (the 35th Perthshire) was formed. We had, however, no headquarters in which to meet, so I scoured the country looking for a suitable hut. It took a long while for me to find what I wanted and I was not at all impressed, initially, by what I was shown at the end of an exhaustive and exhausting day – a somewhat dilapidated henhouse, uninhabited at the time but pretty filthy. After examining it, however, I found that it was in relatively good condition – cleaning it up and painting it would present no problem for Scouts. This is just what they did, and it looked as good as new when they had finished.

The first meeting in the new H.Q. took place on 31st January 1944, and we were nearly turned into icicles! We had a quick word with Eddie

Stewart, the school plumber, and he almost immediately provided us with a second-hand stove: we could now pass tests and attend parades without our teeth chattering. Each patrol had its own corner and the Bulldogs, Foxes, Ravens and Eagles vied with each other to be the best patrol. A silver cup was presented by Mr Palmer Douglas but, rather curiously, I do not think his son, John, joined the Troop.

Our first camp was held in the grounds of Butterstone House, Dunkeld, where I had previously camped with the Ardvreck Troop. Not all dreams come true, but the one I had about camp sites did. We were situated beside a burn and within easy reach of the drive leading to the 'Big Hoose' where our hostess, Miss Crabbie, lived with her friend Miss Lambert. They were both exceedingly kind to us. Miss Crabbie was a most remarkable and very sporting lady. It was rumoured that she was in the habit of shooting deer from her bathroom window – but I have, of course, no proof of that! Both she and Miss Lambert made life almost too easy for us. One day they arrived in their bright yellow Rolls Royce to deliver boxes of what I can only call 'delicacies'. On another occasion, they brought us some powdered chocolate; I do not think it could have been obtained in the U.K. at that time – we were told it came from Canada and was a gift from the Canadian W.R.I. Why we were considered worthy of such generosity we never found out, but we accepted the gift with the greatest of pleasure and the chocolate made our Camp Fires even more enjoyable. We had a good camp. Perhaps Peter Maclellan did not enjoy it very much as he had a bad attack of earache one night, but the others – Michael Anderson (with his white mouse), Anthony Service, Ian Miller and Dougal Bell – enjoyed themselves and contributed a great deal to the success of the first camp of the 35th Perthshire Troop. Dougal Bell was a very practical Scout – what you might call 'a Scout for all seasons'. One day whilst struggling at school with his Latin prep under my supervision, he began to whistle. When I reprimanded him, he replied: 'Well, sir, a Scout is supposed to smile and whistle under all difficulties'. He won that round!

Camps continued to be held at the end of every summer term, though I have to confess that we often sneaked away a few days *before* the term officially ended. For many years, we chose a different site each summer. This was certainly more adventuresome than going to the same site every year but it presented difficulties and, latterly, with kind permission of the Duke of Atholl, we went every year to Banvie Bridge, just above Blair Castle. A better site could not have been found, once one had got used to the flooding of the burn and the maddening midges. On one occasion the Troop was flooded out and had to return to school, but the midges, though they sometimes drove us crazy, never succeeded in driving us home.

It might be of interest to describe briefly some of the camps we attended prior to our settling at Banvie Bridge. I am not likely to forget the one held beside the River Tummel. We did not risk bathing in the river itself, but in a kind of backwater which, though safe enough, provided one could swim, was rather deep. I announced one day that no-one was to go in until I blew my whistle. Possibly one boy was a little *dur d'oreille* – anyhow, he did not wait for the whistle and dived in. He got into difficulties right away and, clad only in a shirt and wrist-watch, the Scoutmaster, at great personal risk, rescued the little blighter. I remember having to do much the same thing on another occasion, when Michael Gardner got out of his depth, but I was not wearing my watch at the time!

The camp held at Fortingall beside the River Lyon was one of the most successful we ever had and the site one of the best. During the summer the river was quite shallow and the boys were able to paddle about at will, without close supervision. It was a most picturesque spot and the river nearby was spanned by a beautiful bridge. The inscription on it intrigued us: *Archibald Ballantyre. His work 1793.*

We were anxious to find a site close to the school suitable for weekend camps, so we chose one in the Birch Park – a wood just above the school – though we sometimes wished that the route to it was not quite so steep. Unfortunately, there were some inquisitive cows that liked the look of the site and this was sometimes rather embarrassing. We tried to curb their interest by putting fences around the tents, but this only partially deterred them. We too liked the site, initially, but after we had spent a night on it we found the ground very hard and uneven. There were two patrols on one occasion – the Antelopes and the Bears – Douglas Boyd being the P.L. of the former and Christopher Kunhardt of the latter. We had a visit from the non-Scouts on the Sunday and, very shamefacedly, had to admit that the demonstration joint we had cooked on a spit was inedible and that we were still hungry! The wood was ideal for Wide Games, the most popular of these being 'Opposite Numbers', such activities being followed, perhaps, by a walk to Loch Broom and a bathe in its icy waters. Had the Scoutmaster participated in this he would have remembered the fact!

Hugh Bodin was the only Troop Leader we ever had; not only was he a First Class Scout but an excellent P.R. man. When we wanted to camp in the grounds of Dunfallandy House we briefed Hugh to approach the proprietor, Mr Stewart-Fergusson, and by his charm and diplomacy he succeeded in his mission. Later Mr and Mrs Stewart-Fergusson took part in the ceremony of the presentation of our Colours, which were prominently displayed in the Scout Hut. We were grateful to them for the gift of a delightful Australian thumb-stick, but unfortunately someone later broke into the hut and stole it.

One of Hugh Bodin's last achievements was the construction of a monkey-bridge across the dam at the bottom of Peggy's Field. Believe it or not, this dam was once deep enough to be used as a mini-marina for model yachts. Hugh was engineer-in-chief of this operation, and it was a great day for him and for all the members of the Troop when they crossed the bridge without getting wet.

Both Douglas Strachan and David Lovelock were First Class Scouts and set their mark on the Troop. David was a natural leader and became Head Boy: without being bossy or aggressive, he got the best out of the boys. Eventually he became a schoolmaster and joined the staff of Cambus-doon Preparatory School, Ayr. Sadly, he lost his life when canoeing.

What impressed me about the P.L.s at this stage of the Troop's development was that the majority of them were perfectly capable of running a parade themselves and, in fact, did so from time to time. Incidentally, I have always thought it a great achievement for a boy of twelve or thirteen to gain a First or Second Class badge, as it involves a great deal of work and dedication. However, not all can become First Class Scouts, so we tried to make each boy feel that he had a useful job to do and that the whole Troop would benefit by his being a member of it. Because of its structure and its inclusiveness throughout the world I do believe Scouting has a valuable part to play in the development of a boy – particulary so in the case of a non-athletic boy – and that it is a very good adjunct to the normal school curriculum.

Those who attended the camp for Patrol Leaders at Faskally House, Pitlochry, had a very profitable time. Duncan McDiarmid, Gordon Fraser, Jeremy Moon and James Sime enjoyed the training sessions under the Assistant International Scout Commissioner, Jack Stewart. A number of foreign Scouts were present, one being a Belgian, André Heintz, with whom we became very friendly. Many years later his son came to see us and we spent an enjoyable time talking about his family's involvement in Scouting.

There were many advantages in securing a permanent site for our camps. When we camped in the grounds of Blair Castle, we found ourselves in the heart of Scouting; International Jamborees and Jambor-ettes were held there and Scouts from all over the world attended. We were very impressed by the Norwegian Troop and by the lay-out of their site, the wooden archway they had made at the entrance to their compound being most attractive. Little did we realise at the time that we would be linked with a Norwegian Troop and that Rupert Lanchester would take some of our Scouts out to Opdal, Norway, to camp with those Norwegian boys. In spite of the language barrier we seemed to be able to get through to them – they were so friendly. This also applied to the Icelandic Troop.

John Duncan, as one of the chosen few to go to Norway, had a rather embarrassing experience on the first stage of his journey. With his head held high and wearing his Scout uniform, complete with the old-type wide-brimmed Scout hat, he was walking down Princes Street, Edinburgh, when one of the city's famous gales suddenly erupted, blowing off his hat. The sight of a small boy tearing down one of the world's best-known streets, chasing his runaway hat and only just catching up with it before it reached an oncoming tram, caused a great deal of merriment to all but the owner of the hat, who must have been hugely embarrassed. However, worse was to follow. The route began at Harwich and ended at Oslo, and for 36 hours poor John lay on the deck unable to eat anything. All he wanted was to be left alone. Luckily, the discomfort was soon forgotten once the ship berthed. The Jamboree was a great success, and when it was over the members of the Scottish contingent were invited to the homes of the Norwegian Scouts, where they were given a royal reception.

At one of these Jamborees, held in the grounds of Blair Castle, we had the opportunity of meeting Jack Stewart again. He was an exceptionally gifted man and as Scottish H.Q. Commissioner (International) was doing excellent work for Scouting at home and abroad. I had never before met a Scouter who could run a camp-fire as he did. Though everything seemed to be spontaneous, the programme was, in fact, very carefully planned, involving most if not all of the members of the Troops present. I still remember the song he immortalised (and acted): 'So we'll put the damper in and we'll take the damper out but the smoke goes up the chimney just the same'. In a very short time he had several hundred boys joining in, singing and making the appropriate gestures. The contributions made by those from abroad (particularly the Norwegians) seemed incomparably better than anything we could offer, but we did our feeble best and received polite applause.

We think back to 1948, when Rupert Lanchester arrived at Croftinloan. Knowing how well he had run the Ardvreck Troop, I was more than happy to hand over to him the management of the Croftinloan Troop. New ideas and methods were needed and I was glad to serve under him for a while as A.S.M. Many Old Boys have spoken of the enjoyment they got out of Scouting when 'Lanky' was S.M. When the Scout Association awarded him their Medal of Merit for his services to the movement, we all felt that this was an award which he had really earned.

Accidents at Scout camps were few and far between. The road leading up to Banvie Bridge, where the Troop camped at the end of one summer term, was very rough and stony. One boy, cycling down to Blair Castle and possibly going too fast at the time, fell off his bike, knocking himself unconscious. He was rushed to hospital and we were very worried about him for a time. It took several days for him to recover, but he is alive and well today and his head does not seem to have been permanently damaged!

I return to the matter of taking risks. It was our practice to allow the prefects to go off on their bikes on a Saturday afternoon during the summer term. We talk rather glibly about taking 'calculated risks', but *we* were doing the calculating on behalf of twelve- and thirteen-year-olds. All they were asked to do was to let us know where they were going and to return at the stated time – they were not specifically asked to behave sensibly, as it was assumed they would, and I cannot remember that they ever let us down. Nevertheless, with today's hazards I would do more than hesitate about letting boys make use of the roads, unaccompanied by an adult. Those lower down the school did, in fact, have bicycles, but when going beyond the school bounds were accompanied by a member of the Staff. I suppose we took an even greater risk when we sent off prospective First Class Scouts on their weekend 'journeys', but there again, circumstances were totally different from those of today. These journeys were most valuable in that they made the boys more self-reliant and better able to cope with unforeseen difficulties. Just as important – they really enjoyed themselves!

CHAPTER 22

MUSIC AND ART

Several Old Boys have said that it was at Croftinloan that they developed a love of music. It heartened me to hear this but it did not surprise me. With Stuart Dewar, Edward James and Rupert Lanchester on the Staff it was not difficult to enthuse boys, as all three masters were musically minded.

One of the first things we did was to form a Gramophone Club. At its height we boasted of nearly fifty members, but attendance sometimes varied: on one occasion the secretary, Michael Philip, minuted that Mozart's *Sinfonia Concertante for Violin and Viola* had been played to a listening public of two – the secretary and myself! Normally, however, the meetings were very well attended. I have one musical regret: the Minute Book, containing the history of the Gramophone Club, together with a great deal of interesting information, has been lost.

We allowed, but did not encourage, boys to read their books as they listened. I was never too happy about that, as music – certainly classical music – deserves one's full attention and should not be regarded simply as a pleasant background; but that is a personal opinion and, admittedly, an old-fashioned one. Anyhow, it was preferable for boys to attend these sessions hearing, if not listening to, music than for them to stay away.

We had a fairly comprehensive record library built up over the years and we tried to satisfy all tastes. Some Overtures were very popular – particularly the Overture to *William Tell*: if there was only time for part of it the boys would opt for the last section, in which the music becomes almost deafening. Children do not change much! Strauss Waltzes were also very popular, as one would expect, but perhaps it was a little surprising that quite a number enjoyed opera (in small doses). One boy completely fell in love (if that is not too strong a word) with *La Traviata*, as I did earlier. *The Drinking Song* was his favourite aria. I sincerely hoped that we were not instilling (or distilling) within him something other than a love of music, and was quite relieved to hear him say lately that he had lost his first love of the opera and never played the record!

Richard Yarrow wrote to say that he was at Ballyoukan at the time when the records of the Beatles were very popular and that Edward

James allowed the boys to listen to some of them after they had gone to bed. Similarly, Rupert Lanchester, whose piano (like his old raincoat) was part of him, would leave the door of his room open so that the strains of a Chopin nocturne or a Beethovan sonata could drift through to the nearest dormitories. Anything modern was anathema to him.

None of those who comment on their enjoyment of music at Croftin-loan fails to mention the truly wonderful machine which reproduced this music. I only wish it were still in my possession: although no beauty it was a joy for ever! Let me describe it briefly. I will not insult it by giving it the generic name of 'gramophone' because it was in a class of its own. Old Boys still speak of it affectionately. Manufactured by E. M. Ginn of London, the first thing you noticed as you gazed at it in astonishment was its enormous horn – not the small horn associated with *His Master's Voice* but a gigantic one made of papier-maché. It would not have liked to have been confined to a bungalow such as ours today but, fortunately, we were able to position it in spacious surroundings at Croftinloan. It lived, in fact, in what we called the Morning-Room, where the Gramophone Club originally met, though later on Club meetings were held in the projection-room of the Assembly Hall.

You might well wonder what was so special about this musical instrument – I know it was not quite that but I always think of it in those terms. I do not suppose I will be believed by some purists or musicologists when I say that its reproductive qualities were very nearly, if not quite, the equal of any instrument one can buy today. In those days there was, generally, a good deal of surface noise when playing a record and using steel needles. With this machine fibre needles were used, which had to be cut before playing a record (and sometimes more than once). Today, everyone seems to be in a hurry and probably would object to the time spent carrying out this tiresome task. I can assure you it was well worth it, as the sound that issued from that horn was unbelievably pure.

Perhaps a footnote would be of interest. When in London I used to make a bee-line for E. M. Ginn's premises off Oxford Street. All the records he sold were of pristine quality. In most gramophone shops one was allowed then to play over the record one thought of buying, but Mr Ginn would have none of this: his customers must receive their records 'fresh'. I am told that one of his assistants started up a similar business on his own account. Rather dishonestly, I thought, he called his business E.M.G. Ltd. – the title used by his former employer. When challenged about the impropriety of this he is said to have replied: 'I don't know what all the fuss is about. E.M.G. stands for "English-Made Gramophone"'!

We were prepared to go a long way in search of music. Our nearest centre was Perth, but the attendance at concerts was so poor that fewer and fewer were given there. However, we did hear Paul Robeson, the Vienna Boys' Choir and the Scottish Orchestra in the City Hall. Normally, though, we went to Dundee where we heard Solomon, Eileen Joyce, Yehudi Menuhin, Carl Schnabel, and had the shooting-brake not broken down we would have heard Infantino – a name not all that familiar to concert-goers, but I had heard him in *Rigoletto* at Covent Garden and was very impressed. I thought the boys would like the style and voice of this distinguished tenor, but we met our Waterloo just outside Dundee, and by the time the fault was repaired it was too late to proceed to the Caird Hall.

We often went to concerts in the Usher Hall, Edinburgh. There was no Forth Road Bridge in those days and queueing up for the ferry could be frustrating and time-consuming. However, it was worthwhile going any distance to hear *Messiah*, Cortot, Cyril Smith and Phyllis Sellick, Claudio Arrau and others. It meant a late return to school and some inattentive pupils the following morning, but the pleasure these performances gave us outweighed any disadvantages. Apart from these musical pilgrimages we used to go to Glenalmond, at the invitation of their Musical Society. There we heard a number of up-and-coming musicians, such as Nina Milkina and Michael Rolls, who were to become internationally famous.

The fact that my grandfather was something of a connoisseur in the world of Art may not seem very relevant here, but I think it is. When, as a boy, I used to stay in his large Glasgow house, I admired his very fine pictures, many of which had been on display at international exhibitions. Whether I cast covetous eyes on them at that time I do not know – but surely I must have thought that, whilst the walls were amply big for hanging them, the light coming through the windows of a town house did not do them justice. When I inherited a few of them I had no such problem. As you can imagine, the light of a country mansion in Perthshire was excellent. Some of the pictures, however, needed to be cleaned and reframed. This work was carried out over a number of years and the transformation was most noticeable. I felt that I had a certain amount of responsibility as an inheritor to look after these works of art, yet necessity made me act rather irresponsibly, you might say, on more than one occasion. One O.C. (who is an art dealer) was genuinely shocked when I confessed to having sold a very fine painting – but I wanted to go to Australia to visit relatives and, as far as I know, he did not! He was quite right, of course, but there are occasions when one has to act against one's instincts.

Young people are often accused of being unaware of, and therefore unmoved by, the beauty all around them, but this accusation has been disproved over and over again. If reading, listening to music, learning to play an instrument, being encouraged to visit picture galleries and so on are part of the family set-up, then the child has a flying start. Nevertheless, I have seen young people from many different backgrounds being very moved and even enthralled when listening to music or examining a work of art.

It is encouraging to hear O.C.s saying that, looking back, they realise that they were, unconsciously, affected by the pictures at Croftinloan and, perhaps more consciously, by the music they heard. Nick Bawtree says he hopes that the harbour scene is still hanging in what was then the school library, and goes on to describe it in great detail. I have not had the courage to tell him, until now, that it is no longer there, but I am glad to be able to soften the blow by informing him that another fine seascape does hang in its place above the mantelpiece. Nick then says that when his attention wandered during the Sunday evening service he would gaze at the harbour scene masterpiece. There is no need to be apologetic, as the seascape possesses equal powers of distraction. It depicts a fishing-boat (could it have been called *La Bonne Espérance*?) battling its way across a wide and dangerous-looking expanse of ocean. If future generations, in moments of inattention, receive inspiration from looking at this picture when they are supposed to be concentrating on the school service I shall be perfectly satisfied! Incidentally, Nick thinks that his love of the sea and of boats may also have been fostered by another picture, featuring a boat seeking shelter in a storm.

Drawing and painting were taken very seriously at Croftinloan and several boys won awards in local and county competitions. Peter Bourne was exceptionally talented and continued to do well in the art world: some years ago he founded a School of Art in Aberfeldy where he runs courses for both mature and aspiring artists.

We have had some very capable art masters at Croftinloan, but I would like to single out Allan McArthur, who also taught at Pitlochry High School and at other schools in the area. We were fortunate in being able to secure his services, for he was a first-class artist and a good teacher. I shall always remember the magnificent back-drops he painted for the school plays, encouraging the boys in such a way that they were made to feel that they were doing most of the work.

CHAPTER 23

FOOD

In wartime, and for quite a long time thereafter, there were, obviously, many restrictions – particularly as far as food was concerned. It is an interesting commentary on the human species that when soap was rationed there was hardly a murmur of complaint! Sweets, rather surprisingly, were not rationed until 1942 – if Hitler had appeared on the scene at that time he would probably have been lynched. But food is a different matter and the shortages hit us pretty hard. Critics of school food, therefore, had a great opportunity of voicing grievances, which were sometimes justified. In those days, and later, we held weekly prefects' meetings, when boys could raise any matter which was on their minds – including food! Any complaints were taken seriously but it was not always possible to remedy them: so much depended on the ability of the cook and how she dealt with the food put before her. After the War, we had a marvellous cook who really spoiled us. She must have thought that she was cooking for a 5-star hotel! If the word 'economy' was in her vocabulary she chose to ignore it. She, naturally, was very popular with the boys and they were not the only ones to enjoy the pancakes she turned out (or over) on Mardi Gras; she was a charming person but found it difficult to work to a budget. Other cooks we employed seemed to be able to cook really well and more economically. One such cook was Nellie Canon, who kept us very well fed for many years and, even after she got married, often returned to help us out, temporarily. Like Barkis in *David Copperfield* she was always 'willing' and seemed to be always smiling. Sometimes, when it proved impossible to replace a cook who had left at short notice, my wife would turn to me and we would say almost simultaneously: 'What about Nellie?' It was not simply her cooking that was so good but the manner in which she accepted responsibility, sometimes under very difficult circumstances. Her attitude had a powerful effect on those who worked with her. Unfortunately, she and her husband and family eventually moved house and went to live in a remote Highland glen – so, 'willing' though she still was, distance proved to be an insuperable obstacle.

Criticism of school food has been a popular pastime from time immemorial. I did once hear of a school where a boy actually admitted that the food was 'quite' good! That was high praise. The furthest one O.C. would go was to say that wartime food was 'interesting', probably quite an accurate description but capable of many interpretations. In the days of scarcity rabbits had, literally, to run for their lives! They soon got to know that Edward James was an excellent shot. The boy who complained of being presented more than once with the rib-cage served up with carrots and watery gravy may have wished that Edward was *not* such a good shot. . .

I think it was on V.J. day that many boys said they had the best meal they had had for years, but where the food came from I do not know, as shortages continued for a long time. I remember that some parents could not get a meal of any kind at Fishers Hotel, Pitlochry, but that may have been due more to bad management than a shortage of food. The previous evening my wife and I entertained two friends in the same hotel so, possibly, we had strained the hotel's resources!

An event took place at one time which could hardly be described as wildly exciting, but it was to make a great deal of difference to the gastronomic life of the school: we welcomed Mr and Mrs Bain from Tomintoul, and the hundred or so hens which accompanied them received an equally warm reception. The birds, which they pampered and fed so well, made a magnificent response, providing us with a valuable source of food at a time when eggs were very expensive and difficult to obtain. I expect the hens laughed all the way back to the henhouse when an officious inspector from the Ministry of Food arrived one day to inform us that our hens were producing more eggs than was legal! I had a brief but pointed word with the gentleman and am happy to report that he departed, if not with his tail between his legs, at least with egg all over his face. . .

A good story often has a bad ending. Mr and Mrs Bain left Croftinloan and I became responsible for the welfare of the hens; I now had horses *and* hens to look after and grew less fond of the latter than I had been. The winter of 1947 was the coldest for 65 years and, as we had very heavy falls of snow, riding became impossible. The horses had to be exercised on a long rein, which was tiring work, and co-operation between man and beast was minimal. After our winter of discontent spring came as a benediction.

We seemed to have become an easy target for the authorities, with the Ministry of Food once again on our tracks: this time we were informed that we had been eating too much meat. This accusation may have been true. How we could have obtained extra rations I have, of course, no idea, but I do know that our suppliers during and after the War were generous to a fault. We were fortunate in having a vegetable garden, but Willie Watt had been called up and we needed more help. The purchase of an M.G. cultivator cut out much of the heavy work.

I do not suppose that many knew much about what went on in the kitchen – apart from the lucky few who received 'titbits' from a generous cook as they stood, hopefully, at the kitchen window. Hamish Carlton says that he had a special relationship with the cook (I am quoting him!) who was also referred to as 'The Queen'. Apparently he had a propriet-ary interest in a most co-operative hen which, very conveniently, laid its eggs in the grass-box of the motor-mower; this was housed in the summer-house near the classroom where he was supposed to be work-ing, so Hamish could hear when his hen laid an egg. When it had laid three, he took the eggs to the kitchen window and tapped on it. 'The Queen' opened it, took the three eggs and, silently, exchanged them for three freshly-baked ginger biscuits. The lovely taste of those biscuits has, he says, remained with him to this day.

It would appear that Hamish and his friends were not too well fed at Croftinloan, or was the reason for their behaviour simply that they were hungry for adventure? Anyhow, they decided to supplement their diet and this is how they went about it. After the Staff had had their evening meal, the 'left-overs' were put on a trolley just outside the dining-room. As soon as the boys in the dormitory above heard the rattle of the trolley, they tip-toed downstairs to see what they could scrounge. They imagined that the Staff was quite oblivious of what was going on but now, on looking back, Hamish has his doubts. He is fairly certain that the 'blind' eye which every schoolmaster possesses (or should possess) was brought into operation. On one occasion, Iain Laughland dropped the lid of the vegetable dish (a knock-on?) and it fell with a clatter to the floor. For a moment he and his accomplices were frozen to the spot – then, hearing no response, they scampered back to bed. It was bliss indeed to do so, undetected, with a warm roast potato wrapped up in a handkerchief to be consumed at leisure!

CHAPTER 24

WELCOME VISITORS

During the War years and just after, we welcomed a number of lecturers and entertainers to Croftinloan. It is not possible to mention them all, but some were outstandingly good. Frequent visits were made by Seton Gordon, writer and naturalist; Edward Broadhead, Dickens impersonator (who did his make-up in full view of the audience); Col. Badcock, who gave some witty and useful advice on the training of dogs. When asked whether he could recommend a book on the subject he replied, somewhat to our surprise: 'The Bible is the best book I know and, particularly, the Book of Proverbs'. On being asked to explain his choice, he replied: 'The verse I find most appropriate in that book is: "Understanding is a well-spring of life to him that hath it",' and then he added with a smile, 'I like these words, "to him that hath it"!' That incident reminds me of a question put to Edward James by a parent whose boy had done very badly in the Common Entrance Scripture Examination and who was going to arrange for him to have some coaching during the holidays: 'What book would you recommend, Mr James, on the subject?' Edward replied very graciously and without a flicker of a smile: 'I think the Bible is the best book available'.

As an entertainer, Hubert Leslie was in a class of his own. With a face to match his art, his visits were always looked forward to. He was blessed with a very large, somewhat aquiline nose. One of my earliest recollections of him is of his balancing a peacock's feather on the end of his most prominent organ and walking across the Library: a peacock's feather was, in fact, his trade-mark. He was a most delightful man and was welcomed at many schools throughout the country. Because of ill-health, he had to discontinue his work in 1952, after forty years of giving so much pleasure to several generations of young people. Fortunately, he found time to write *Artful Art and Breathless Brainwaves* – a book to which I periodically return to revive very pleasant memories.

Captain Knight would, I think, have been lost without his golden eagle. There was certainly a quite extraordinary rapport between them. When the pair arrived at Croftinloan there was no difficulty in finding accommodation for the Captain, but where were we going to put his

mate? 'I expect you have an outhouse near the main building which is
empty and can be locked', he suggested. Fortunately, we had. 'But what
about food?' I asked. 'Oh, I have brought that with me', replied Capt.
Knight. He then proceeded to show me what the eagle lived on. I wished
I had not asked! My question prompted him to open a small suitcase in
which he carried his pyjamas, hairbrush, shaving-tackle etc. and, wrapped up badly in an old copy of *The Times*, a revolting lump of red meat. The
outhouse proved to be secure, and my wife and I spent an amusing
evening listening to some of Capt. Knight's experiences; the conversation
did not lag but it was a little one-sided. The following day, the lecture
began with a request: might the owner of this magnificent bird have
permission to release the eagle? With some slight and understandable
hesitation I granted this. The boys waited, goggle-eyed, to see what
would happen. We had no sound reason for our fears, but one does not
meet an eagle every day at close quarters. To see a golden eagle hovering
over the heads of boys in the Library was a strange sight indeed. When it
had completed its flight it returned, obediently, to its master. Later, we
met the eagle again, though not in the flesh. A film had been made called
I know where I'm going, featuring Capt. Knight and his eagle, and we all
trooped along to the local cinema to see it. The film was very good but we
were rather disappointed that the pair appeared only briefly.

Mr George Cansdale, a former curator of the London Zoo and a
lecturer and broadcaster, with Percy the python and Polly the bush-baby,
became very popular with the boys. They were invited to handle the
python, but those who accepted the invitation did so rather apprehensiv-
ely. Complete silence was called for before the rather timid bush-baby did
its act. This consisted of introducing itself to the boys by leaping from
shoulder to shoulder along the rows, after which it returned to its owner.

Mr Cansdale had a very amusing story to tell about Percy. Whilst
lecturing in Lancashire he found himself in an hotel where there was no
heating of any kind. Fearful for Percy's welfare, he put him at the bottom
of his bed, where his feet could keep him warm. As he was leaving early
the next morning he left Percy in the bed whilst he went for breakfast.
When he returned to his room he found the bed stripped and no python
to be seen anywhere. Spotting a pile of dirty sheets in the corridor he
rapidly felt through them, and there was Percy curled up in one of them.
Mr Cansdale never took that risk again and always kept a hot-water
bottle in his luggage. Had the chambermaid seen the python when
stripping the bed she would probably have had a heart attack!

Perhaps the most dramatic demonstration ever given at Croftinloan
was when Commander Thomson R.N. visited the school to illustrate how
a diver goes about his business. Dressed in his diving gear, he produced
a terrific explosion to show us what really happened when a submarine
had foundered in the Thames. A bolt could be fired through the hull of
the submarine to provide fresh air for the trapped crew. The gun required

was massive. The diver had a one-inch thick piece of metal through which he could fire the bolt. In reporting the tension building up in the audience, one O.C. reports that no-one thought the Commander was going to do what he said he would do. He made elaborate preparations, supporting the metal on the edge of the stage, then – one, two, three, and there was an earth-shattering bang which made the boys almost jump out of their seats. When the dust had settled it was seen that the diver had been true to his word: there was the bolt right through the steel, both glowing red-hot. The Commander then proceeded to unscrew the cap, triumphantly. That corner of the stage had been compressed to a good two or three inches, the only tangible reminder over the next few weeks of an amazing incident.

CHAPTER 25

'GLADLY LERNE, GLADLY TECHE'

Croftinloan's record as far as the Common Entrance Examination is concerned was extremely good over the years, yet not so very many scholarships were gained. Many were examined, but few were chosen! It was noticeable, however, that many of the 'also-rans' often later out-stripped boys who had been successful in gaining awards. This might sound like criticism of the quality of teaching at the preparatory school stage but that would be unjust as, for the most part, the members of the Croftinloan teaching staff were dedicated and well-qualified school-masters. It is, of course, so easy to make excuses when scholastic successes are rather thin on the ground; I am cheered, however, by a recent article in *Prep School* in which the writer criticises the scholarship system in terms with which I would largely agree. He concludes his article by remarking that, in his view, the time has come to put the scholarship giant to sleep in the interests of all our schools. Nevertheless, I think he would probably agree with me that it is good for the really bright boy who needs 'stretching' to have a higher goal than the C.E.E. standard, always provided that he is not called upon to curtail or abandon activities or subjects which he enjoys but which are not, in the strictest sense, examinable.

We are not particularly proud that we hold one record we can never lose! I shall not bother you with the background of this tale, as it probably only interests me, but the bare facts are as follows. The 'hero' of the tale, by the way, had a rather distinctive name, so I shall call him 'John'. He was a pleasant boy but did not have a very settled family life, and some of his actions were symptomatic of his upbringing. He had been entered for Eton and duly took the entrance examination. I do not suppose the invigilator was aware of what was going on under his nose, but he could have done nothing about it had he known – he was, in fact, presiding over an event which would most probably never occur again. The completed papers were sent off to Eton and we awaited results with some trepidation, though we thought John would have done just well enough to scrape through, as he was by no means a dull boy. We were certainly not prepared for the letter that arrived a week later informing us, as politely as possible, that John had not scored a single mark in the Latin paper. On a former occasion, apparently, an entrant had gained 1% in the Latin exam, but John had smashed the record! It came to light later that he had no intention of going to Eton, and the only way in which he could achieve his aim was to 'spoil' his paper.

One of the events we pretended to look forward to was the school inspection carried out by H.M. Inspectors of Schools. In retrospect, we did quite enjoy this, but though we told the boys there was nothing to fear, I suspect that members of the Staff felt as jittery as they did. In those days I do not think the inspectors knew a great deal about the running of a preparatory school, but they were quite skilful at trying to hide this! In point of fact, we learnt from each other. Two inspectors stood out as being most helpful. Dr Dixon put the boys at ease almost as soon as he entered the classroom: he won them over by saying that although he was a linguist, he was going to examine them in Geography (possibly the geographer was off sick), adding that even though he did not know a great deal about the subject, they would be able to enlighten him . . . The boys were now more relaxed and gave some very sensible replies to his questions. The other inspector had the name of Crippen, but fortunately that meant nothing to the boys. He was a mathematician and, like Dr Dixon, knew how to handle boys and make them feel at ease. Some of the answers to his questions, however, were pretty disastrous. Is it a nervous reaction that compels less intelligent children to rush in where angels fear to tread and offer to answer questions put to the class generally?

In those early days, a report was sent to us by the Scottish Education Department and, greatly daring, we used to send copies to the parents. Then the reports stopped coming and we wondered why. I wrote to the Department and was told they were no longer being sent out, as it was often so difficult to read the writing of the inspectors who had submitted them – surely a case of 'tongue in cheek'! The final decline resulted in the inspectors not coming at all, except to make sure that Johnny had sufficient cubic feet around his bed to enable him to develop satisfactorily. On one occasion an inspector told me solemnly that we had more wash-hand basins in the school than was legally necessary!

On the whole, we were sorry when the inspectors ceased visiting us. They had been friendly and helpful, and they certainly kept us on our toes.

CHAPTER 26

'TO SEE OURSELS AS OTHERS SEE US'

Charles Vaughan-Johnson recalls that once when some boys were playing on the north drive a van came roaring up, shot round the side of the main building and screeched to a halt at the back door, despite the notice which read: 'Please drive slowly'. The Headmaster dashed out of the house just as the young driver was getting out of his vehicle. According to Charles, the H.M. was very angry. 'You are either a very brave man or a fool', he shouted, 'Can't you see that there are children all over the place? You could easily have knocked one down'. V.J. (as he was normally called) and the other onlookers thought that the driver was a brave man for risking the wrath of the H.M., and a fool for driving as he did. Unfortunately, V.J. continues with another story which puts me in a much less favourable light. He reports that we were returning from some outing or other and several of the 'privileged' (as they thought) were permitted to drive back with me in the shooting-brake, which never went slowly if it could help it! Driving along Loch Tayside on a winding, downhill road, the speed increased considerably (to put it mildly). The boys hung on tight, but were relieved when the speedometer dropped to a sedate 70 m.p.h. '"Sorry about that", said the H.M., "I got cramp in my accelerator foot and couldn't slow down". We thought of the van driver – but there was a difference . *We* were all *inside* the car!' concludes V.J.

Richard Yarrow reported that 'Bronze' (one of my more polite nick-names) was considered to be rather fierce at times and had a reputation for driving fast cars and possessing an equally fast temper. There seems to be supporting evidence for this assessment. One of the senior boys was entrusted with the task of operating the school projector for the regular Saturday showing. On one occasion he ran a few frames through to check that all was well and then pushed down the reverse switch – a thing he frequently did, as the film could be hilariously funny when run backwards. Now it so happened that a good many projector bulbs had blown recently. (In those days they cost around £5 each.) Anyway, all was ready, the lights were put out and the screening began. For a few seconds the screen remained blank. Had another bulb blown? No, but the projectionist had failed to switch over to the forward position. The

Headmaster exploded and the operator was not in favour for some time to come . . .

Another explosion apparently took place some time later, when the H.M. discovered that persons unknown had in some way 'disfigured' the pristine appearance of the new block of lavatories, which was his pride and joy. Frank Gerstenberg remembers cowering in a corner of the changing-room as an irascible schoolmaster came striding through, scattering toilet rolls in all directions. Perhaps those who witnessed this unseemly outburst discovered that day that their Headmaster was human after all!

Fortunately, the growth of Croftinloan was not wholly dependent on a somewhat mercurial Headmaster. Not only was he blessed with a Staff which, for the most part, was bound up with the welfare of the boys, but over the years he was fortunate in having had a number of boys whose service to the school was outstanding and who, after leaving Croftinloan, distinguished themselves, not always in spectacular ways but in a manner which influenced those who came in contact with them. Some have already been mentioned, but here I would like to put on record the contribution which several others made both at Croftinloan and after they had left.

Aulin Baird's home was near Basingstoke, but he was fortunate in that his grandparents, Mr and Mrs Alasdair MacGregor, live not far away from the school – at Cardney, near Dunkeld – and close contact was kept by them. He was also fortunate in being, initially, in Miss Roma Stewart's class. She had a very high opinion of Aulin – indeed we all had, as he moved up the school, for he was a boy who threw himself wholeheartedly into whatever he did. It is, however, of what he achieved after he left school that I would like to write. I am grateful to his mother, Mrs Sladen, for giving me the following details.

In 1963 an article appeared in the press under the title of *Vanishes at Sea*. Very few details were given, but it concerned Aulin Baird, son of the late Squadron-Leader Greville Baird (who was killed in action in 1943) and of Mrs Baird.* Aulin was one of a crew of five and was last seen clinging to the wreckage of the U.S. schooner *Windfall*. A Belgian crew tried to rescue them but was beaten back by a gale and 30-foot waves.

During his short life (he was only twenty-five at the time of his death) Aulin did a great deal for the World Wildlife Fund, and his many friends made a contribution to this organisation as a tribute to his memory. In so doing, they wrote as follows: 'Because Alasdair Aulin Baird exemplified, during his four-month sojourn in America, the qualities of courage, character, friendliness, love of nature, integrity and charm, and was such an effective representative of international understanding in every aspect, we, the undersigned, whose lives he touched at one point or

* Later Mrs Sladen.

another during his stay, have made this contribution in gratitude for the pleasure each one of us had in knowing him'.

Aulin's mother received a letter from Buckingham Palace, under the signature of Rear-Admiral Christopher Bonham-Carter, which read as follows: 'His Royal Highness, the Duke of Edinburgh, has received a remarkable tribute to your late son from one of his friends in America, Mr Lawrence Smith, who informed him of your son's interest in the field of world conservation of wild life and of the great impression made on him and on his circle of acquaintances by whom his tragic loss was deeply felt. These people have banded together and as a memorial to your son, have handed a cheque of some 780 dollars to the World Wildlife Fund in the United States.

'Mr Lawrence Smith particularly asked that His Royal Highness should cause you to be informed that this memorial had been established as a tribute to your son and this His Royal Highness has instructed me to do.'

John Forsbergh (Duff or Duffy to his friends) came to Croftinloan when he was six years old. He had never known a happy, settled family life, though his American grandparents were devoted to him, but they were elderly and distance made it impossible for them to come to the U.K. as often as they would have liked. Duff suffered severely from asthma but refused to let this handicap overcome him. He was invariably cheerful and, wherever he went, he spread love, warmth and good humour. After leaving Croftinloan he went on to Dollar Academy, where he died at the age of fifteen. We shall never forget his lack of self-pity and his consideration for others; we had lost a very good friend.

We have many happy memories of James Sime, who went on to Gordonstoun after leaving us. He came of farming stock and lived near Dundee. He looked like a young Greek god and was a natural athlete. When a ball was placed at his feet or in his hands he would do the most incredible things with it. He was tragically killed on his father's farm when a fork-lift truck came in contact with an overhead power cable. Apart from his athletic skills he had many fine qualities, combining toughness with gentleness.

CHAPTER 27

OUT AND ABOUT

As the school was situated in an area of historical interest, we thought we should know something more of the events which occurred there in days gone by, so we started off near the north entrance to Croftinloan. Crossing the road, we entered an enclosure the ground of which was very overgrown, but it was just possible to see the remains of St Catherine's Church, surrounded by gravestones. This area was called 'The Fourich', a Gaelic word which I believe means 'The Fort of the Careful Watch', and dates back to Pictish times.

Farther north and just short of Moulin is Kinnaird Cottage, in which Robert Louis Stevenson stayed with his wife Fanny during the summer months of 1881. A plaque was inserted in 1928 in the garden wall of the cottage, commemorating his stay. He was charmed by the views and the scenery, but his health prevented him from staying there for long.

We went across to Aberfeldy, immortalised by Rabbie Burns for its 'birks and braes'. All around this area are evidences of the work of that remarkable Irishman, General Wade, who was responsible for building bridges and making some fine arterial roads. It was he who asked if the soldiers whom he employed could be called 'The Black Watch'. The bridge over the Tay at Aberfeldy, which is a fine example of the General's architectural skill, was built in 1733, when Wade was Commander-in-Chief of the Forces in Scotland. I do not think he would have approved of the traffic lights fairly recently erected, but the bridge is so narrow that they were really required.

Then we went on to Fortingall, where just before reaching the village we saw the famous standing-stones which are considered to be the best in Britain, with the exception of those at Stonehenge. On our return journey we went into the church at Logierait and saw the mort-safes and unusual tombstones there: in times gone by (and perhaps today) the dead had to be protected from the living. It would have been difficult then, if not impossible, to steal anything from a grave so well protected from 'body-snatchers'. The gruesome aspect of this appealed to some boys – the more sensitive turned away in disgust!

If there are many evidences of the activities of General Wade, there are even more of those of Prince Charlie. He is supposed to have spent a night at Moulinearn by the River Tummel: possibly one of our Old Boys – Michael Barr – whose parents occupied the fine old house (once an inn) might be able to tell us whether that is more than a supposition. Queen Victoria is also supposed to have slept there, but she had a remarkable facility for sleeping almost everywhere in Scotland!

On other occasions we visited Blair Castle, Scone Palace and Glamis. As the laird of the latter castle was an uncle of two of our boys, we were given a private viewing. I do not know who it was that showed us over, but she was economical with words and this helped us to remember a good deal of the fascinating story she had to tell us.

We also paid a visit to the site of the Battle of Killiecrankie. The boys already knew something of this battle (which took place in 1689), but what interested them more than the cause and effect of the engagement was the site where a desperate soldier, running for his life, jumped across the Garry at its narrowest point (16 ft.) without being able to take a run at it. It would seem to have been an impossible feat but later it was vouched for by the soldier who achieved it, when he returned with General Wade.

The famous solitary standing-stone in the village of Moulin had a functional use long ago. It stands in a field below Baledmund House, where it was said the Moulin Market used to be held. Apparently, those who had concluded a deal would clasp hands in front of this stone to seal the transaction. This stone is also said to have been associated with Druid worship.

I have heard it said that 'The Queen's View' was so called long before Queen Victoria saw it. As she herself stated that her name had been given to a view she had not seen we must take her word for it! She was in Scotland in 1844, but it was not until 1866 that she saw the autumn colours around Loch Tummel at the spot we so much enjoy visiting. It was reported that she 'posted north to Croftinloan in 1865, making through Edradour to Glen Briarachan and Strathardle'. Be that as it may, an important but less well-known event took place when John Rollason and five of his friends set off on their bicycles to see the Queen's View. There they met some Americans, touring Scotland, who seem to have been charmed by the cyclists and asked them to stand beside their bikes whilst they photographed them. John says that thereafter they had a very friendly conversation, and describes the incident as an American version of *l'entente cordiale*. I hope they found time to look at the view!

CHAPTER 28

THE LIGHTER SIDE OF SCHOOL LIFE

Young people are in the habit of saying just what they think and because
their intentions are not normally malicious, they get away with it. The
remarks which amuse me most are those which I remember with relish a
long time after they have been made – often they are not hilariously
funny and cause me to chuckle rather than guffaw. Children are not
choosey as to time and place, and delight in exercising their gift of
humour in the classroom. Parents would, I think, be horrified to know
how frank young people can be about their home life. This can be
embarrassing to the schoolmaster (or schoolmistress) who often tries,
usually unsuccessfully, to change the subject. 'Sir', said one persistent
boy to me, 'My father's an awful swank'. I pretended not to hear but
when the accusation was repeated I felt I had to say something: 'Oh no,
I'm sure he isn't' – 'Oh yes, he is', insisted the little pest, 'He's always
talking about how good he was at everything when he was at school'.
    There is no doubt that if a schoolmaster, or indeed anyone who works
with young people, lacks a sense of humour and of the ridiculous, he is
unable to meet children on their own ground. As a matter of fact, I have
met few who are deficient in this way. It is, of course, more difficult to
answer questions asked in the classroom, where there is an audience,
than to give a reply to a child when he is alone; nevertheless some
questions are always difficult to answer. When a small boy quoted his
father (who was an Army Officer) it was not too difficult to give a tactful
answer: 'Daddy says Hitler has bitten off more than he can chew. What
do you think, sir?' But when a child asked the Assistant Matron: 'Miss
Wallace, do you intend to have twins when you marry?' I can quite
imagine that Miss Wallace ('Wally', as she was affectionately known)
would reply in such a way that the child would not be likely to repeat the
question! Being noted for the delicious toffee she made, she would quite
likely have 'bought' him off with a piece.
    It has already been mentioned that Miss Berwick was, in the words of
more than one Old Boy, a 'substitute mother'. She was particularly good
with New Boys and seemed to know just how much sympathy to give
them when they were feeling homesick. She assured Geoffrey Crerar

that, once he settled down, he would like being at Croftinloan. 'Never!' he replied, indignantly. 'My sister is the oldest member of the family and she is the one who should have gone to boarding-school'. Three weeks later, Miss Berwick heard loud guffaws coming from Geoffrey's dormitory and on entering found that the poor little homesick boy was responsible for them. 'I told you you would soon be happy', said Matron, triumphantly. However, Geoffrey had an answer to that: 'Don't think that I am happy because I am laughing. I am *not*.'

Probably the most oft-quoted joke is the one for which Charles Drew was responsible when, I think, he was a New Boy. I was outside in the school yard when I heard my name being called; the call seemed to come from a distance and at first I could not locate it. When I did, I saw Charles Drew, some thirty yards away, beckoning to me. I stood my ground and, in turn, beckoned to him. Rather reluctantly, he proceeded slowly in my direction. At this stage, I must say, I was rather puzzled at Charles's behaviour but I was soon enlightened. Holding some orange-peel in one hand, he said, politely, 'Please, sir, would you put that in the waste paper-basket?'

The lighter side of school life keeps breaking in. I had been showing some rather taciturn parents over the school and, finding the going rather hard, I asked them if they would like to meet some of the boys. Without any obvious enthusiasm, they indicated, coldly, that they would. I was to regret making the suggestion. Some of the boys were on the playing-field, so we stationed ourselves at the top of the steps leading down to the field. The first boy to arrive was Nigel Bruges. Commander X wasted no time. 'Do you enjoy being at Croftinloan?' he asked. Generally rather talkative, Nigel must have thought that such a question deserved a short answer. 'Not particularly', he replied and walked on. Did the Commander see the wink Nigel gave me? Anyway, he went away to look for a vacancy elsewhere.

Who said that small boys were so scared of their masters that they kept their mouths shut when dying to voice their thoughts? Edward James was teaching Maths and had written the answers to the set problems on the blackboard. He then turned to Christopher Kunhardt and asked him if he had been able to solve all the problems. 'Yes, sir,' he replied, 'but not all my answers are the same as yours'.

Scripture and History seemed to be the two subjects presenting the best scope for making howlers. One of the questions asked in a Scripture paper was, 'Who were the Magi?' Hew Grant was heard to mutter, 'Maggie? Who on earth is she?' It would be easier to answer this question today!

I do not know what Mrs Nicholson's reaction would have been had she heard her son, Hamish, remark in class, 'Sir, my mother is twenty-seven years older than Munro'. As we all knew the latter's age, we knew the rest! Another boy, not to be outdone, informed the class that he had seen

Hugh (my son) the day he was born, adding proudly, 'before his eyes were open'!

Two rather out of the ordinary questions were once put to me. When I was teaching I was taken aback to hear a boy remark, plaintively, 'Please, sir, would you keep quiet? I can't think'. I thought of Gerald Moore and of his book *Am I too loud?* I had been taught a lesson! The other question was perhaps apocryphal. Roger Brown reported that when he had been summoned to the Headmaster's study to receive a pep talk before entering the big, bad world of Public School and University he took the initiative. Before the Headmaster could open his mouth he asked, 'Is there anything you would like to know, sir?'

Patrick Barty (the boy who in a history examination described the Mace as a 'glorified truncheon') recalls that after lunch boys were instructed to lie flat on their backs whilst the Headmaster read to them; he says he never found out whether the purpose of this inactivity was to help the digestion or to enable boys to repent of their past. Sometimes, the humour of the reading appealed more to the Headmaster, says Patrick, than to the listeners, but it was diplomatic to laugh occasionally. It made him think later of Goldsmith's *Deserted Village* where we read: 'Full well they laugh'd with counterfeited glee, At all his jokes for many a joke had he'. Patrick did not go on to say that he and others had 'learn'd to trace The day's disasters in my morning face', but I expect they did.

Christopher Woods, whose home was in Dorset, complained in later life, when he had time to look back, that no-one had prepared him for the barbaric culture he was going to enter when he left England's green and pleasant land for Scotland's dark, Satanic moors. His brother, Ian, not to be outdone, complained of having to endure the torture of eating 'mealy puddings' which made him feel sick. Christopher was equally disgusted when porridge was placed under his nose with salt in it. Had sugar been available, as some sort of palliative, it would not have been so bad but there was none in sight, so he just had to shut his eyes and gulp down what the Scots had the audacity to call porridge!

Letters, written on Sundays, could be quite amusing. Members of the teaching staff supervised the writing of these, suggesting items of interest and helping with the spelling when asked, but were told never to read the letters, so the boys felt they could say what they liked. One of the mothers, however, showed me a rather amusing letter she had received from her son. It consisted of one paragraph and read as follows: 'We had a cricket match yesterday. We won even though the farthers [sic] could slam the ball. I have been to see the Queen Mother on Wednesday. George Cansdale came last night He brought a snake and a bush-baby. He is coming for the evening service in a few minutes. We are only allowed to write letters on Sunday'.

Many amusing incidents occurred when rehearsing the French and English plays. One especially stands out in my mind. Bill Bruce and

Dougal Bell were acting in a play which I think was entitled *Romans on the Dee*. As Roman soldiers, they had to sit on a classical wall for quite a while – declaiming their lines in front of parents and visitors. They *both* completely forgot their lines and had to ad-lib until the curtain came down. Fortunately, they were boys who were rarely upset by anything and neither was ever at a loss for words when not acting; I wonder if any of the parents realised that they were listening to two actors of great originality. The spontaneity engendered by the loss of memory seemed to improve the play, and Bill and Dougal got a great reception.

In taking part in *The Crimson Coconut* Hamish Carlton recalls that he was obliged to kiss his girl friend (John Duncan) whose identity, even with two tennis balls up her jumper, lipstick in the usual place, and wearing a skirt, could not be concealed. He says he gritted his teeth and went through with it!

The following incident occurred during the holidays; I expect that the boys were very envious of John Duncan, as he was the only Croftinloan boy to witness the embarrassment of the Headmaster. I had been invited to John's home at Roehampton for a day or two and *Cinderella on Ice* was currently playing at the Empress Hall (directly behind the Earls Court Exhibition Centre then, but now non-existent). I was taken to one of the performances. As John's father was a director of the Empress Hall Ltd. we were honoured by being given very good seats at the front. Little did I realise at the time that my proximity to the ice was to be my undoing. I was permitted to enjoy the show for quite a time – that is, until one of the mischievous Ugly Sisters decided that I had enjoyed myself long enough. Skating across to where I sat, she imprinted a smacking kiss on the top of my bald head. The make-up left behind could be seen by most of the spectators, who did not seem to have any consideration for my feelings. I do not think I have ever brought the house down before but I certainly did that memorable night! My handkerchief was incapable of removing the Ugly Sister's outrage and all I could do was to pretend that I was thoroughly enjoying this addition to the general performance.

Once upon a time we had a kitchen-man of the name of Cowie. He complained to me one day that there was what he called 'a lack of hilarity' in the kitchen and felt that he would have to leave our employment. Later, he must have found something to laugh about as he changed his mind and withdrew his notice. I do, however, sympathise with him as, having had to work in the kitchen when we were short-staffed, I found it one of the most difficult places in which to raise a smile, let alone a laugh!

It may seem rather strange to consider this as a humorous story but as some of the boys who witnessed the incident thought, initially at any rate, that it was hilariously funny, I have decided to include it here.

One day, on arriving at Croftinloan, I thought that the car was not behaving quite as it should. Whilst the engine was still running, I opened the bonnet to see if I could locate the fault. I was certainly living dangerously. A finger came in contact with the fan which very nearly sliced it off – the longest one on the left hand. I rushed into the school, holding a handkerchief under the mutilated finger so that, if the tip did fall off, I would be able to prevent it from falling to the ground. My finger dripping with blood, I asked the first boy I met if he knew where the Matron was. He thought that this was just another of the practical jokes which I was too fond of playing and roared with laughter. Though I tried to assure him that this was no practical joke, I did not wait to find out whether I had convinced him or not but tore upstairs and found my way, somehow, into the Medicine Room where the Matron (my sister) plied me with brandy and then attended to the finger. I can tell you that I blessed that brandy! To cut a long story short (or to make a short finger longer) the school doctor re-united the tip with what was left of the finger. The fact that he too thought the whole thing a huge joke may have been part of the psychological treatment he was in the habit of giving his patients, but I did not appreciate his apparent lack of sympathy. However, I had learnt a lesson and went easy on practical jokes for some time.

The following story had a happy ending. I had driven my car up to the front door and was intending to collect my wife, who was in the school. I waited for quite a while, but as she did not appear and I was in a hurry, I stepped out of the car very quickly and went indoors. A little later, I found my wife, who told me she would be ready in a few minutes, so I said I would wait in the car. When I opened the front door I was astonished – the car was nowhere to be seen! I rushed back into the house, found my wife in the kitchen and told her that I thought the car had been stolen and that I was going to phone the police. We both went outside, very puzzled indeed, and looked around for the car, but it was still nowhere to be seen. Then I caught sight of it, stranded some 25 yards away in the middle of a bed of azaleas . . . What had happened was this: when parking the car at the front door I had not put the brake on, as I should have done, even though the ground appeared to be dead level. In getting out of the car I must have given it some impetus and, with the brake off and being on a slight slope, the car started to move. It ran backwards across the courtyard, went down a very steep slope, just avoiding an oak tree, then down a second steep bank, and finally came to rest in the azalea bed. We were absolutely dumbfounded.

Some three miles away there was a garage run by an Old Boy of the school. I knew that he would have equipment which could get me out of an embarrassing situation, so I had to swallow my pride and tell him the whole story over the phone. He listened politely but I cannot imagine what he thought. In due course, he arrived and took stock of the situation, then asked me to get into the car and steer whilst he pulled it up the two steep banks. I got in, but the experience of being in a practically vertical car was too much for me, so I decided to steer it up the second bank from the outside. Eventually we reached the top. Clive Bridges asked me if I had put the brake on: I had not! And the car? It did not even have a scratch on it – a small piece of azalea was all I could find under the body. I was glad all the boys were away on an outing when the car set off on its own as if remotely controlled, but they were most disappointed at having missed such an unusual spectacle. For days it was the talk of the school!

CHAPTER 29

RECOLLECTIONS OF OLD BOYS AND MUSINGS OF ONE 'OLD BOY'

Ian Purvis and others write to say how much they enjoyed the Scripture Union meetings held every week at Croftinloan and particularly the talks given by James Beveridge, the General Secretary of the Scripture Union in Scotland, during his frequent weekend visits to Croftinloan. He was exceedingly good with boys and believed that it was important to get to know them both before and after he spoke at our Sunday evening services. David Lamb, now an architect in Johannesburg, says that it was as a result of one of those talks that he became a Christian.

Nick Bawtree is grateful for a practice which I do not think was all that popular, saying that what he was asked to do every Sunday morning before setting off to church was the most precious heritage he received from his time at Croftinloan. He is referring to the thirty minutes set aside for the purpose of learning selected verses from the Bible. He thinks he must have learnt a thousand. Nick will be interested to hear that a few years ago I received a letter from one of our more senior Old Boys (Bill Bruce), asking if I would send him a list of these verses. Unfortunately, I did not have a list but manufactured one from memory, hoping he would be satisfied. I certainly was, for it was good to know of his continuing interest. Some Old Boys will remember a scheme, called 'Search the Scriptures', which really did involve searching. Boys who wanted to participate were given a list of texts on a gummed slip and they had to find the correct references. When they had found six or so, they stuck the slip into a small notebook and were then given the next six verses. One boy said the scheme taught him how to find his way about the Bible.

Another boy writes to say that the lengthy sermons given by the minister of Moulin Kirk had a rather soporific effect on him; he was impressed by the fact that the minister arrived at church wearing a top hat. Another boy remembers the talks he used to give to the young people. I wonder if he remembers those the Rev. Charles Hepburn gave on the Seven Dwarfs. Each Dwarf in turn would accompany him into the pulpit, and each one got his message across rather effectively, I thought.

It is good to know that Anthony Maclaurin and Rob Brown had fond memories of what we, euphemistically, called the Salon – the less sensitive would have simply called it a hut. However, once it had been painted red, white and blue (inside!) and matching curtains put up, it went a long way towards deserving such a name. The furniture was scarcely Louis Seize, but it was functional and adequate. As it was sited some distance from the classrooms our singing and general brouhaha did not, I hope, disturb others. Competition, however, arrived in the shape of a language laboratory and the Salon became passé. Many boys seem to have enjoyed the fun and games we had in it. It now lives nearby *en retraite*.

William Scarlett comments on the fact that the New Boys (or 'New Bugs' as they were called) naturally knew nothing about school rules and had a wonderful time breaking quite a number of them; they arrived a day in advance of the old hands to enable them to settle in more easily. The boys were kept very busy and made to feel that the work they were given to do was essential if the school were to open the following day. They had a whale of a time running up and down the banks and behaving as irresponsibly as they could without actually starting a revolution. However, the honeymoon did not last long and they had to toe the line once the main party arrived. William has lost none of his tact: he reports that he did a minimum of work at Croftinloan – except in the French class! Now, in Brazil, he speaks fluent Spanish.

James Ball (an American boy who lived in London) presented his own version of *Macbeth* – in modern dress, of course – perhaps not quite as good as the original version but certainly much funnier. He himself took the leading role, and the audience gave him and the supporting cast a noisy but appreciative reception. When he asked in a strong American accent: 'What these weird things are I know not. What they mean I am none the wiser. Pray let us continue. This is not the kind of weather to stay talking in', he brought the house down. James's attempt to form a baseball team was not so successful. The formation was the easy part: the difficult part was to get fixtures with other schools, as no other prep school seemed to play the game. The team had to go into liquidation but James continued to entertain us. He did a great deal for the school and we remember him for the delightful boy he was.

Alasdair Cockburn has a certain number of complaints to make. He resented being bowled when tying up his cricket boots, but was a good deal more resentful when bowled by his father in the Fathers' Match. How his father reacted when he heard that his son described him as 'a most incompetent cricketer' I can only guess! Alasdair recalls having been punched in the face when playing against Blairmore. That must have released something in the psyche of the two forwards, as they are now firm friends. Alasdair evidently had a strange effect on people. As a new boy, if you please, he hit a senior boy full in the face with an acorn: the victim took no retaliatory action!

Hamish Carlton seems to have been accident-prone. He managed to break his nose when playing Rugby. The surgeon told him that he could have his new nose either on the right or the left side of his face but not in the middle: he opted for the right, as those who know him will realise. The second accident took place when playing against a school for which he does not seem to have unbounding admiration. How many degrees his nose was moved I do not know, but it seems to have settled down for the time being. He adds, further, that he still has the scar on his right hand caused by a saw which slipped from his grasp: he had to receive several stitches and was the hero of the hour. In spite of these accidents, he appears to have regarded his stay at Croftinloan as a happy one and describes the school as a place where the boys were encouraged by a friendly and understanding staff. Hamish remarks that it does seem strange that having qualified in Law and worked in Hong Kong; the Middle East; Japan; U.S.A.; Iran; Libya; Indonesia etc. he should decide to make his permanent home only a few miles from Croftinloan. He has one boast – he was in the Rugby team which was captained by Iain Laughland.

Our sick-room (which had originally been used as a night-nursery) had a very lovely frieze on the wall. It remained in mint condition for many years – a fine tribute to the boys who had to occupy the room for a while. Even when it began to look a little worn around the edges it still gave a great deal of pleasure to the patients, and to parents who had come to see their boys. Jeremy Moon describes the figures on the frieze as 'medieval huntsmen, cavorting all round the place'. I dare not contradict him as I did so once before and was proved wrong – I now make a public apology! One day he told me, very excitedly, that he had seen a kingfisher on the banks of the river Tummel (or even in it). I pooh-poohed the idea and said he must have been seeing things, which is more than likely! However, an interesting article appeared recently in our local newspaper. In an attempt to lure back the kingfishers and other birds to the rivers of this area, willows are being planted by the R.S.P.B., and who should be photographed planting the first tree beside the river Leven but an Old Boy of Croftinloan – David Erdal.

Patrick Barty recalls that when playing Rugby he was constantly being told (and even threatened with all kinds of penalties) to 'get low'. It took him at least a term to understand what that meant. He is proud of the fact that when travelling to an away match he and other members of the team were allowed, by courtesy of the guard, to travel in the guard's van as far as Dunkeld. There they were met by Mr Killick of Clifton Hall School, which had moved from Edinburgh to Amulree for the duration of the War. Patrick thinks the Headmaster must have been able to purchase some petrol on the black market, as he was able to take our team back to Dunkeld, where a train was boarded for Pitlochry.

Charles Vaughan-Johnson sampled Croftinloan both as a boy and as a temporary junior member of Staff after coming out of the Navy. I am glad he does not say that the days spent at Croftinloan were the happiest days of his life. I am always sorry for anyone who is obliged to say that. What he does say, however, is that his years at Croftinloan were the happiest of his *school* life.

We have very pleasant memories of Bill Gordon (nickname 'Weasel' or 'Belette'). He proceeded to Glenalmond where he became a school prefect: he was the first winner of a travelling scholarship awarded on character and influence. Bill says he had an aptitude for doing badly in examinations, yet he obtained an honours degree in Mechanical Engineering and is an M.I.C.E. and M.I.Mech.E. He has worked in many countries, became a Strategic Consultant with the MAC Group, and now lives in France. He speaks of the family atmosphere at Croftinloan, saying that his memories centre around members of Staff and referring to the 'soft' Miss Berwick (I make bold to correct a fluent French speaker but would not *'sympathique'* be a better word?). He then speaks admiringly of Miss Fieldhouse, who did so much for the school, of the 'amiable' Paddy Laird, the 'solid and wonderful' Rupert Lanchester and the 'dedicated' 'Sid' James. I shall always remember the day on which Col. and Mrs Gordon came to see over the school; Edward joined us as we went round. I had, previously, told the parents that we had no immediate vacancies. After our tour of the school, Edward turned to them and asked if they would like to see the Boiler Room. I imagine they must have thought it rather a curious question – but possibly they had previously, unknown to me, been talking about central heating. At any rate they went off with E.M.J. and were back in the hall in a matter of minutes; I then told them that I had looked again at my Entry Book and found that I could offer them a vacancy for their son. I may say I never regretted that decision, as Bill turned out to be one of the best boys we ever had.

I was also proud of another similar decision. After seeing round the school the parents concerned appeared to be pleased with what they saw and said they would like to send their son to us. I said I would very much like to have him but there were no vacancies. 'Nonsense', said the father, 'that's what they all say. When does next term begin?' He had worn me down and how glad I am that he did: the boy contributed an enormous amount to the well-being of the school and we were more than sorry when the time came for him to go to Uppingham.

Quite a number of Old Boys refer to their experiences at Ballyoukan Lodge, rented by the school in 1948, which helped us to tackle more easily the problem of accommodation. Some will remember Mr and Mrs Macaulay, the first caretakers: Mr Macaulay played the pipes and read a chapter of the Bible every day but not, I think, simultaneously! He also had a spittoon in the kitchen but, fortunately, he had a deadly aim. (I hasten to add that the boys did not have any meals at Bally.) Mrs Macaulay was famous for her wonderful head of hair: it looked like an enlarged bird's nest and the boys said that they would not have been surprised if a bird had emerged from it! The Macaulays were succeeded by the Scotts. Mr Scott was so small that when driving his car he had great difficulty in seeing the road ahead of him. One day he asked me if I could let him have a cushion which I no longer needed, so that he could place it on his driving seat. He had a passion for tidiness and used to award prizes for the tidiest dormitory. They were a cheerful and co-operative couple.

CHAPTER 30

THE LAST LAP

For many years the only building available for such events as plays, lectures and concerts was a converted laundry, referred to earlier. It was not difficult, therefore, to decide how best we could celebrate our Semi-Jubilee. Mr Tommy Thoms, a Dundee architect, who had two boys at Croftinloan, drew up plans for a hall, which had to be within close proximity to the school. One parent was extremely generous, and his donation in response to the Appeal enabled us to make a much earlier start on the building than we had anticipated. Indeed we were most grateful to all parents for the interest they showed and for enabling us to reach our target in a comparatively short time.

In order to clear the site for the foundation to be laid, a large sycamore had to be uprooted. As the stump proved to be impossible to remove by mechanical means, it was decided to use explosives. We were rather alarmed at this decision as the offending stump was very close to the main building. However, the contractors were well known to us and they assured us that no risk was involved, so the explosives were placed in position and we all made our way indoors to watch from the dormitories. An employee of William Duff and Sons was given what seemed to us rather a dangerous task – that of setting and lighting the fuses. He was a gentleman of uncertain years but this was probably routine work for him. His appearance was not very prepossessing and he was distinguished by having only one (visible) tooth! I had known him for years and looked upon him as an old friend. We were all rather dubious, however, about his ability to handle explosives, though I knew he was a good mason: could it be that he at one time had had an accident – hence the one tooth? However, it was too late to stop the proceedings. We hoped and prayed that he would not blow himself to bits. When all was ready he lit the fuse and then backed away but oh! so slowly – he seemed to be courting disaster. I had taken up a vantage point in one of the top dormitories as I wanted to get a ciné shot of the operation, but was laughing so much that I had great difficulty in holding the camera steady. Our single-toothed friend reached safety only a few seconds before the gelignite exploded. Whether his slow retreat was due to the fact that he had tripped over some object or other I do not know, but I am glad that my ciné-camera was not a video as the language which floated up to the dormitories was anything but choice!

The boys felt they were helping to make history when they inscribed their names on the foundation bricks. Unless the building is destroyed by fire or laid low by a hurricane these names will forever be concealed, but no doubt the Old Boys will tell their children and grand-children about the impression they made when they were at Croftinloan.

The Assembly Hall was opened in 1961 by the Warden of Glenalmond, Mr R. M. M. Barlow, in the presence of over three hundred parents and friends. It was most fitting that Mr Barlow should have been asked to perform the ceremony as not only had he and his predecessors extended help and friendship to us over several years but also because many of our boys had gone on to Glenalmond. In the chair was Lt-Col. Andrew Nelson who, after serving on the Board for some years, had become chairman of the Governors in 1960. His wise counsel, patience and flexibility made everyone feel, instinctively, that as long as he was at the helm, our problems would be tackled energetically and solved in due course. Croftinloan owes him a very great deal of gratitude. He devoted a lot of his time to the welfare of the school, going out of his way to get to know the members of Staff, which was very much appreciated.

Now that the Hall had been built we were able to expand our activities more easily. No longer did we have to set up, and later remove, the moveable stage; no longer was the front row of the audience almost *on* the stage; no longer did the actors awaiting their cues have difficulty in finding a place to stand.

I have heard of many good reasons for encouraging children to perform in public but this one was new to me: John Rollason had a strong Yorkshire accent, and writes from South Africa to thank me for helping him to lose it. He was given a part in a play at school entitled *Le Poltron Courageux* and maintains that this enabled him to get rid of his Yorkshire brogue. I am afraid I was a little less complimentary about his French accent then and said so. There was no risk to my safety at that time but later he became Scottish and British Universities Lightweight Boxing champion!

When in 1969 Tony Brain joined the Staff he did a tremendous amount to raise the standard of French and wrote a number of plays which the boys enjoyed acting. We were very sorry when he left us but he found the distance between Farnham and Pitlochry just too great.

Small-bore rifle shooting played an important part in the life of Croftinloan. Mr Jimmy Robertson, who represented Scotland in full-bore competitions on many occasions, coached the boys and we were very fortunate in securing the services of one so skilled. Though quite a number of his pupils did well in the world of shooting after they left Croftinloan, I can only mention two here. Donald Dale shot for the

Scottish Schools against Canadian schools when he was at Glenalmond and later became an international marksman. Nick Bawtree was in the Uppingham VIII when the school won the Ashburton Shield at Bisley. Unfortunately, he did not continue with his shooting but had he done so he would probably have gone far.

Over the years the boys were present at a good number of launches at Yarrows Shipbuilding Yard in Glasgow. These outings were always most enjoyable and the launches themselves (and the lunches!) will never be forgotten. We are most grateful to Sir Eric Yarrow for inviting us to attend these and for arranging such wonderful vantage points for us; I think the last time we were at the Yard was when H.R.H. Princess Anne launched the New Zealand frigate *Canterbury* on 6th May 1970.

A Debating Society was formed at Croftinloan. At the last debate I attended the motion read as follows: 'In the opinion of this house, all schools should be co-educational'. Whether this debate had any effect on the decision to accept girls at Croftinloan I do not know, but the Ayes had it by 12 votes to 9!

In 1965 a house was built for the Headmaster in what was called the Scout Wood. In that wood there stood a lovely beech-tree and under that tree the Scouts were wont to pass their cooking tests. With my knees distinctly wobbly, I approached Scoutmaster Lanchester and informed him nervously of my intention of getting the tree felled. He was somewhat taken aback but tried to make light of the matter. I felt that I was about to perpetrate a crime: to think that I, who had founded the 35th Perthshire Troop, should stoop so low was almost unthinkable! Anyhow, the tree came down, the house was built and peace reigned.

Miss Margaret Green then entered the stage and was destined to play a prominent role in my life and in that of the school. During the summer months she had been running house-parties at Croftinloan for girls (mostly from England) and I had met her on these occasions. She was teaching at Clifton High School at the time, so we were both tarred with the same brush or a similar one. It was mutually decided that it would be a good idea if we were to go into partnership. This decision was to be implemented in 1966. When it was announced at School Assembly that Mr Brown was going to be married to a Miss Green those with a sense of the ridiculous were greatly amused! After we were married my wife continued to teach and became closely involved in many school activities; I have a suspicion that if the boys had been invited to give her a report it would have been a good one.

Just before the curtain fell on this particular play and another began we were entertained by the Old Boys at a local hotel; pleasant remarks were exchanged and we were, generously, presented with a silver salver and a cheque. My wife and I retired in 1971 (as mentioned earlier), so the editor of the *Dundee Courier* was a little late in inserting one of his very amusing cartoons, as it did not appear until 1986. It depicted a Mr Brown (yes, he had got the name right!) being presented with a parting gift, while his workmates stood around, trying to conceal their emotions but applauding, nevertheless. The chairman put everything in perspective when he said: 'Well, Brown, the old place won't be the same without you – that's one consolation!'